YORKSHIRE HUMOUR

Yorkshire Humour

compiled by
Ian McMillan

illustrated by
Tony Husband

Dalesman

First published in 2009 by Dalesman
an imprint of
Country Publications Ltd
The Water Mill, Broughton Hall
Skipton, North Yorkshire BD23 3AG

Introductory texts © Ian McMillan 2009
Extracts © Dalesman 2009
Illustrations © Tony Husband 2009

ISBN 978-1-85568-266-5

Printed by 1010 Printing Ltd

CONTENTS

Acknowledgements

J A, Mrs R V Ackroyd, E J Adkins, Mrs A E Alba, Robert A Alderson, S Allen, Mrs Edith A Appleby, D L Appleton, HM Armitage, L Armstrong, A W B, G B, G H B, T B, G E Bailey, R Bailey, Norman Band, Mrs H W Barber, R Barker, Harry Bateson, Tom D Bateson, John Baxter, Mrs C Beacher, A J Beattie, J Beech, F Beecroft, Mrs P Bellamy, John Bentley, Mrs M Benton, J P Bilsborough, Grace C Bingham, A W Birstwith, A Blackburn, Mrs B Blackburn, John A Blackburn, E Bolton, James E Booth, Nina Booth, C Bottomley, T W Bowyer, J L Bowes, A Brear, A Brooks, Edgar Brown, Mrs Charlott Bruff, Mrs S Bull, From *Advance*, magazine of Bulmer & Lumb, R N T Burke, F Burley, W A Butler, Leonard T Butterfield, J P C, R C, T Caldwell, B Cardus, Stan Cardwell, Jane Carroll, Mrs P Carroll, Phyllis Carroll, J Carter, S Cheesbrough, J Clark, J R Clarke, Miss E Clarkson, Leonard Clegg, Mrs P J Coates, J W Cole, A C Connell, Miss D Cook, R Cordingley, C Crampton, J Crompton, Rhoda Cross, Miss Mary Cussons, T D, A Davis, F G Dawson, Fred Dean, E K Dearlington, Ian Dewhirst, John Dickson, F E Dodson, J Kenneth Douglas, F M Douglas-Kay, W Downs, A Duncan, L E, J M Eames, Sheila Easton, AD Eastwood, Mrs M I Elliott, F M Ellis, T E Elsworth, T Escott, J Fairburn, F Fairclough, Mrs M Fairhurst, Wilfred Fattorini, Mrs E Fell, E Ferguson, K Fisher, Leslie Fisher, H Foster, Harry Foster, L F Foster, Miss Mabel Frank, R Freeman, L Frobisher, T G, M Garth, Miss E Gee, H L Gee in *500 Tales to Tell Again*, Ken Gill, Hilda M Gledhill, Miss Jane Glyde, Alan Gostick, L Greenwood, A H, M H, T H, W H H, R J Hainsworth, A Hall, F Halstead, Adele Harland, R Harper, J B Harris, T Harrison, John Hartley, G Hawksworth, Miss F W Heaton, H Hellewell, G H Hesketh, Mrs S Hill, Walter Hill, B Hind, Ben Hindle, Dennis Hirst, A Holden, Wm Y Holdsworth, Miss M Holmes, R W Hornsey in *Children's Chatter*, Mrs I Horsfall, W M Hudson, J Irwin, E J, E Jackson, Harold H S Jackson, L Jackson, L Jacques, F Johnson, Rev G Johnson, W A Johnson, Will Jones, A K, A R K, T L K, Freda M Kay, T M Kearns, Alice Kelsall, T W Kendal, L Kershaw, Mrs Kiddy, A H Kilburn, Mrs M Kilner, A Kinder, L M King, N Kitchen, W Kitching, C L, J K L, T L, Muriel Lander, J K Laprell, P Lawrence, T Lawson, F Layton, M Layton, Mrs A Leach, E Leatham, Frederick Lee, J M Lee, M Lee, Mrs M Lee, Mrs R Lingard, F Lister, George Lister, L Lister, Mrs Mary E S Lister, T Lister, A M, C M, Mrs F M, J M, J C M, K M, S M, H Mallinson, E Marlow, R Marshall, S Martin, Sydney Martin, F H Marvell, David N Mason, Harold Mason, H McAllister, Mrs I Megginson, L Mercer, Mrs A Miller, Mrs A J Milner, Madge Mitchell, John Morgan, E R Morley, E Morton, Mrs M Morton, J J Mulroy, J F Murphy, Mrs Joyce Mumby, E N, Rev K E Nelson, Mrs C M Newcombe, G Mary Nicholson, F Norman, Mrs S Norman, Margaret Ottley, B T P, E J P, F P, S P, W S Parks, W Pattinson, L Pearson, O Peddle, G E Pickles, C R Potter, David M Pritchard, Mrs M M Pybus, E R, K R, M E R, W R, E Radcliffe, M Ratcliffe, Mrs M D Ratcliffe, J L Rhodes, E Richards, A G Richardson, Ellen Richardson, H Richardson, Mrs A Robinson, N Robshaw, Mrs A Rogan, G Roylance, Mrs Rush, J S, John Wm Scaife, G W Shaw, Leslie Scheftsik, Councillor Brian Short, J W Simmons, Alan R Simpson, J Simpson, Miss D Sinclair, Miss Renee Slinger, Rev Gordon P Smailes, From *The Smith*, house magazine of Thos Smith and Sons, Rodley, Arthur Smith, Mrs C E Smith, Fred Smith, G S Smith, J S Smith, R P Smith, T W Smith, L Smithson, M Smithson, T Somers, Miss J E Sparks, F Sparling, Colin Speakman, R A Stockdale, M Stollard, H G Summers, E T, John T Taylor, R M Tempest, Bertha Thompson, Mrs E M Thompson, M Thompson, Miss Thompson, M Thwaite, Miss A Townson, J W Utley, F W, Mrs J Wade, Mrs E M Walker, Pamela Walsh, Robert S Walsh, Mrs J H Walton, K Walton, L Ward, A Watson, Mrs E Watson, F Watson, J Watson, Miss P M Watson, T Watson, N Webster, Ben Wellock, R West, S West, W White, Miss J Wilcox, A Willis, A L Wilson, Miss J P M Winn, J Winterburn, R W Withers, E Wood, J L Wood, L Margaret Wood, Mrs M Wood, D A Wrangham, William R Wright.

Introduction

This sounds like a made up story but I swear on Fred Trueman's best pipe that it's true. Years ago our doctor's surgery used to be in an old house near the Cross Keys pub. The ill and the snuffling and those grimacing in pain and those wanting a sicknote so they could go fishing in the pit ponds would gather in the front room, sitting awkwardly on settees and kitchen chairs in a tight space that was stuffed with ornaments and family photos. I once turned up with a chest infection, wheezing like a pair of bellows, and I discovered that there were at least twelve people in front of me looking like some kind of Bamforth postcard version of the Last Supper. I slumped on an ancient easy chair and waited.

A man at the other end of the room with a face like a child's drawing of a bloodhound sat rubbing his long face as though it was giving him some cosh. He reached over and rifled through the pile of magazines on the table in the middle of the room, looking for something to distract him. He discarded the *Exchange and Mart* and picked up a copy of the *Dalesman*. He flicked through it. He furrowed his brow as he read a little piece and he stopped rubbing his face. He looked up at the ceiling and I could see that he wanted to laugh, but somehow he thought it inappropriate in a room full of sadness and wincing and noses running like overflow pipes. He gazed deep into space and deep within himself. He fought to stop a smile playing round his lips. He failed. He lost the fight, floored and dazed in the first round. The smile played happily round his lips.

He grinned like a death mask. His shoulders began to shake. Tears began to stream down his cheeks. He waved his *Dalesman* like he was waving a flag of surrender. He tried to bury his face in it. He kept trying to control the laughter but the laughter defeated him. And then, in a room full of infections, the laughter became the greatest and most infectious infection. The woman next to him, in a headscarf emblazoned with the Great Little Trains of Wales, began to snigger. She didn't know why she was laughing but she was laughing and the Great Little Trains of Wales rattled on their Great Little tracks around her shellac perm. An enormous bloke with his arm in a sling began to laugh in a fat monotone like a ship's siren, his mouth opening in a big sloppy O. A little girl who had been weeping and clutching her doll gazed in wonderment at her mother as she crumbled into a howling mass of hilarity, like a female version of the Laughing Policeman made of school custard. The waiting room was transformed from a room that wanted to weep into a room that couldn't stop chuckling. Mrs Harley came in to tell the next invalid it was their turn to see Dr Galvin and she came into a space that was like the concert room of the Bottom Club when they had a good turn on. She looked aghast, her arms folded over her vast bust.

The man with the long face controlled his almost uncontrollable laughter and pointed at the copy of the *Dalesman*, now fallen on the floor like a shot bird. "Ah," said Mrs Harley, in the voice of a sage, "everybody laughs at the *Dalesman*," and she tried a little laugh herself, sounding like somebody grating cheese; oddly that stopped all the other laughter dead like a light being switched off in an empty room.

That story illustrates one of the *Dalesman*'s main functions: to make you laugh. Of course, it's also full of interest and language and a kind of Yorkshire anthropology, but ever since that day in the doctor's waiting room I've thought of it as a magazine that makes you laugh. And if not laugh, snigger. And if not snigger, grin. And if not grin, then make that small and almost imperceptible sideways movement of the head that, in a person from Yorkshire, can signify all kinds of things from

"How are you this fine day my good man?" to "Yes, I thought they played well on Saturday although that second goal was most certainly offside" and "By, that's the funniest thing I've heard since my Uncle Charlie told me about Jack Briggs⋆ falling down that hole at the top of our street."

This book is a collection of all the kinds of humour the *Dalesman* is famous for, a range of humour that, although it's strictly Yorkshire humour, is actually quite hard to define. It's a fact, though, that Yorkshire people are funny. If you need proof, go and stand in a bus queue with a bunch of them, or go to a football match with a carful. Sit with some in the barber's shop. I guarantee funny things will be said or seen.

I'm not saying that there isn't such a thing as Essex humour or Northamptonshire humour, of course. There obviously is, and dozens of examples of comedy from the two counties will be springing to your lips as you read this, won't they?

What's the essence of Yorkshire humour, though? What's the Unique Selling Point? Well, I think there are a few, if you can have such a thing as a few Unique Selling Points. One of the USP's is the language. Somehow Yorkshire Language is in itself funny: ejaculations like EEE (as in EEE she were thin in the old gag) and By and Now Then and Flippin Ummer make you smile. It's a rough-hewn language, a language of opposition to the status quo and a language that the boss couldn't really understand so you could use it to take the mickey out of him and he'd never get what you were on about. What people from outside Yorkshire know as the Yorkshire dialect is of course thousands of dialects, one for every village and two for every street in the county, and this gives us the possibility of tiny jokes that only work in certain backyards in Guiseley. Or, as the old Muker joke goes: "A farmhand was gonging his kikes when a young marrer leaned out of his darrywack and said 'Ho maisster: yer toll-bill's showing!' " I don't get it either, but the people of Muker laugh so much when they hear that one that oxygen tanks have to be on standby. They have to have the special standby adhesive ready, too. That's Standby Gum.

Also, Yorkshire is full of funny place names. Wetwang. Idle. Friendly. Shelf. Booze. The Land of Green Ginger. Jump. The names lend themselves to comedy, whether intentional or not. I'm just off to the Idle Working-Men's Club. Friendly Skins Rule If It's Okay With You. Is this bus going to Jump? Well hold it down while I get on. Somehow I don't think you can get that level of ribaldry from Bexleyheath or Farnham or Solihull.

There's also the weather and the hills; those two phenomena lend themselves to humour, I'm sure you'll agree. Hills can make you gasp and if you're fat they can make you sweat and if you've worked down the pit they'll make you heave for breath, making inappropriate 'mating elk' noises, and if you drop your change it'll roll to the bottom and if you slip you'll tumble all the way down, possibly through crowds of sheep droppings like Colin Cushworth★★ did that time up in North Yorkshire, ending up with dozens of squashed full stops on the back of his cardy.

And Yorkshire weather is just funny, or perhaps our reaction to it is. When it's sunny people of a certain age will still go out in a cap and a muffler and a heavy woollen coat and after a few minutes they'll say: "I'll tell yer what: it's not just red hot, it's white hot." Their umbrellas will whip inside out in the wind, and their caps will blow off like Yorkshire Frisbees. They'll slip in the ice, landing like bouncing bombs on the slippery pavement, and they'll look up to a grey sky in the middle of a downpour and say: "Well, at least it's raining in Lancashire..."

Yorkshire humour. This book's full of it. It'll make you laugh, and it'll make you feel better, like it did to us all that day at the doctor's.

★Not his real name. He may still be alive. Or his relatives might. The ones with the dogs.
★★His real name. He won't mind. You don't mind, do you Colin?

OUT OF THE MOUTHS OF BABES AND INFANTS

*the funny things children say –
schooldays – families*

I was once in Harry Holden's barber's shop having my usual trim; I must have been about seven years old and I was sitting with my mam and a lot of blokes. As usual, I wouldn't stop talking. I was asking the assorted pitmen and retired pitmen and pit top men how you actually got jewels into a watch. "My mam's got a jewel on her ring," I piped, "but it's too big to go into a watch, isn't it, Mr Holden?"

Harry stopped clipping for a moment, holding his scissors aloft like he was tempted, if only for a fraction of a second, to clip more than my hair. "Does tha know," he said to the crowd, "tha's got moor rattle than a can o' mabs." There was general agreement signified by general murmuring; this was the era of children being seen and not heard. Then, from round the room, assorted voices tried to top Harry's image. "He's got moor rattle than ten peas on a drum." "He's got moor chelp than a stuck hoss." "He's got moor words than a teacher's book." "He talks moor than my Auntie Madge, and that's saying summat." "He's got verbal squits." "He's not from a silent order, is he?" Me mam remained tight-lipped; she knew this kind of banter was only the last vestiges of music hall, its embers still glowing amongst the Brylcreem and discarded hair.

I was outraged at the time, and I still am. I talked a lot because I was a kid! Kids are meant to talk! And, more importantly for this book (and for life itself, but this isn't meant to be a philosophical tome) they're meant to say funny things. They're meant to say they like gravy because that's what pirates eat, like my lad said when he was at junior school; they're meant to shout "Granddad, your tail's enormous!" as our Thomas did once in some public toilets, and they're meant to write, as I once saw in a Christmas story in a junior school exercise book in Ilkley: "The wise men came and peed round the door..."

Welcome to the world of Yorkshire childhood: moor rattle than a can o' mabs. And a very good thing too.

Ian McMillan

A teacher at a West Riding school was pointing out that a surname often indicated the trade of the ancestors of those who bore the name.

He gave, as example, Smith, Taylor, Baker and others. Then he questioned one of the boys.

"What were your ancestors, Webb?"

"Spiders, sir."

Overhead in the village shop:

"How did that naughty little boy of yours get hurt?"

Another customer: "That good little boy of yours hit him on the head with a stick."

"Now, Tommy," said the Dales teacher, "let me see how much you know of my lesson on whale fishing. For instance: can we eat the flesh of the whale?"

"Yes," answered Tommy.

"Good boy," said the teacher. "And what do we do with the bones?"

There was a moment's pause, and then Tommy said with determination: "We leave them on the side of our plate, miss."

"Finished, mum!"

Willie had passed his eleven-plus and had just gone to his new school. One day he was in the village shop with his mother.

"And how is Willie getting on at his new school?" asked the shopkeeper.

"He's getting on well," said the boy's mother. "He's learning woodwork and French and algebra. Now, Willie, say something to Mrs Smith in algebra."

When four-year-old Billy attended Sunday school the vicar's wife told them a story about the feeding of the five thousand. When she had finished she said to Billy:

"Now whatever would your mother do if Jesus brought all those people to your house and she only had a little bread?"

Back came the answer: "Oh, Jesus could have the bread and the others could make do wi' teacakes."

The class had been told to draw anything they liked, but when the teacher came to young Johnnie, all she saw on his paper were two upright thick lines and one thin straight line linking each of them.

On inquiring what it was, she was told: "That's a posst and that's a posst, and that's a weshing line."

"But where is the washing?" she asked.

Back came the indignant reply: "Me mam 'adn't getten it done yet."

A schoolteacher set his pupils a past exam paper as preparation for when their turn came. On an outline map of England various areas were lettered and the appropriate answer required. Across the area anciently inhabited by the Brigantes was the letter B.

'Name the tribe inhabiting Area B in Roman times' was the question. And on one answer paper the teacher read the answer: 'The Brontës'.

On a recent Sunday when Luke, aged four, reached home his mother inquired: "And how was Sunday school this morning, dear?"

"Not so good," replied Luke, and looked very serious. "You see, Daniel's in the lion's den again."

It was the Queen's birthday and the teacher in a junior school near Leeds was trying to interest her class in the daily life of the Queen. "Can any of you tell me where the Queen lives when she is in London? It begins with a 'B'."

A bright little girl shot up her hand.

"Please Miss, Buckingham Palace."

"Yes, Mary. That is correct. Now can any of you tell me where she stays when she goes for her holiday? That also begins with a 'B'."

Immediately little Johnnie put up his hand.

"Yes, Johnnie. Where does the Queen go for her holiday?"

"Butlins, Miss."

The schoolmaster in a West Riding school asked his boys to write an essay on 'The Dog'. When the efforts were brought to him, he noticed that two of the pieces of work were word for word alike.

"How do you account for your essay being exactly the same as that by Willie Brown?" he asked one of the boys.

"Well, sir," the boy replied. "You see we were both writing about the same dog."

The teacher, giving a health talk to her class, warned them never to fondle animals. "Can you give me an instance of the dangers of this, Jackie?" she asked.

"Yes, Miss, my Aunt Alice used to kiss her dog."

"And what happened?"

"It died."

9

Amy had been given a bicycle for Christmas. Some days later the local garage manager told her mum she had brought it in to see if he could stop some of the rattles it made when she rode it.

"You know," she told him solemnly, "Santa Claus doesn't make things the way he used to."

A Dales schoolboy's definition of a map: "A piece of paper that helps you to get lost."

A teacher in a Swaledale school had been telling the children the parable of the lost sheep. She asked the children why the shepherd was so pleased and overjoyed to find this one sheep when he still had the remaining ninety-nine in his flock.

There was a dead silence for a few seconds, then one bright little fellow replied:

"Well, miss, 'appen it wor t' tup."

A school class was being questioned about a book which had been set as a holiday task.

"And where did Nicholas Nickleby go to school?" asked the teacher.

"At Dotheboys Hall, near Greta Garbo in Yorkshire," came the bright answer.

In a Dales school, the lesson that afternoon was on Russia.

At the end the teacher asked the class to tell him what they called the ruler of Russia.

"T' Tsar," they all replied.

Then he asked what they called his wife.

"T' Tsarina," they answered correctly.

Finally he asked what the Tsar's children were called. There was no reply until a tiny voice at the back called out: "Tsardines."

"I want to complain about the bike you brought me last year."

It was a very appetising school dinner, but no second helpings were available. A young 'hopeful' receiving this news sadly remarked: "If there's ivver owt good, there's nivver nowt left."

A Dales schoolmaster, impressing on his pupils the need to think before speaking, told them to count fifty before saying anything important, and a hundred if it was very important.

A day later he was standing with his back to the fire when he noticed several lips moving rapidly. Suddenly the whole class shouted: "Ninety-nine, a hundred – your coat's on fire, sir."

The infant teacher in the small village school was having trouble getting through to one of her pupils, a boy who was particularly dense. After re-phrasing her question three or four times not a glimmer could be seen on the boy's face. So in desperation she finally asked: "Well, what does your father say to your mother first thing in the morning?"

Quick as a flash and happy to have understood her at last, he blurted out: " 'E says get off your be'ind and get summat done."

Will is not enthusiastic about history. The other day he returned home in a very disgusted state. "Grandpa," he said. "Were you told about Alfred the Great when you were at school?"

"Yes," he said, "but that was a long long time ago. Why do you ask?"

"Well, they're still goin' on about him."

A Skipton woman washed her baking tins, then left them in the hearth to dry. When her four-year-old son asked why, he was told that it stopped them going rusty.

Next day the child had a bath, and was being dried in front of the fire when the vicar came.

"Getting dried where it's warm?" asked the vicar.

"I have to," replied the little chap. "It stops me going rusty."

A boy from a Dales farm was visiting an aunt in Harrogate. As she summoned him to the table prior to beginning the meal, he eyed his side plate with misgiving.

"Don't you have plates at your house?" asked his aunt.

"Aye," the lad replied, "but not wi' nowt on."

"Now, Willie, you must not be selfish. You should let your brother have the sledge half the time."

"Yes, mother," replied the boy, "I do. I have it going down the hill, and he has it coming up."

Father was at the edge of Bempton Cliffs admiring the sea below, the sandwiches clutched in his hand. His son approached him from behind and tugged his coat.

"Mother says it isn't safe there," said the boy, "and you've either got to come away or give me the sandwiches."

The leader of the Brownie troop asked each little girl what good deeds she had done at home since the last meeting. Each told of washing the floors, dusting the furniture and making the beds. Finally, the leader came to Jean.

"And what did you do to help?" she asked.

Jean looked solemn as she said:

"I kept out of mother's way."

Passers-by in Dewsbury were moved by the sight of a seven-year-old girl solicitously leading her younger brother by the hand across the busy road. The boy's eyes were tightly closed.

"What's the matter?" a man asked sympathetically. "Can't the little fellow see?"

"Oh, he's all right," the little girl assured him. "We do this every Saturday when the sun's bright. That way, when we get inside the movies he can open his eyes and find us two seats right away."

"Don't ask!"

"Isn't Spot a naughty dog, Mummy? He ate my doll's slipper."

"Yes, darling. He ought to be punished."

"I did punish him. I went to his kennel and drank his milk."

During a spell of severe weather, a Yorkshire boy was of necessity confined to the house with elders similarly imprisoned. The result was a good deal of free advice for the solitary child.

"Be observant," said his father. "Learn to use your eyes," said an uncle. "Don't go through life like a blind man," said an aunt.

Several days afterwards the family conclave asked the child if he had learned anything interesting as a result of their advice.

"Oh yes," replied the youngster calmly. "Father keeps a bottle of whisky behind *The Pilgrim's Progress* in his bedroom, Aunt Jane has a wig, and Uncle George goes to the Black Horse when the rest of you are in bed."

It is told of a certain church dignitary that he once discovered some small boys seated in a ring round a dog, in the corner of a field.

"What are you little boys doing?" he inquired.

"We're having a competishun," said one urchin, "and whoever tells the biggest lie wins this 'ere dog."

The cleric thought to improve the boys, and began: "When I was a little boy I never told untruths," but was interrupted by a voice which cried: "Give the gent the dog."

Said little Betty to her mother: "Don't wash my face today, mummy, it's got a smile on."

A little boy had to apologise in a letter for forgetting his aunt's birthday. So he wrote: "I'm really sorry I forgot your birthday. I have no excuse and it will serve me right if you forget mine next Friday."

"Mother, mother, Tom wants half the bed," came the cry from upstairs.

"Quite right, my dear; let him have it."

"But Tom wants his half in the middle, mother."

A very dignified and correct lady came upon some little boys bathing in a pond in their birthday suits. She was horrified.

"Little boys," she called, "isn't it against the law to bathe here without suits on?"

"Yes," replied a freckled urchin, "but Johnny's father is a policeman so you can come on in."

The 'veteran' of the Second World War had been telling his son of his experiences in the great conflict, in France, Italy and North Africa.

When he had finished the small boy asked: "But why did they need all the other soldiers, dad?"

A Halifax father promised his son that if he passed his exams he should have a bicycle as a reward. The boy failed, and there was the inevitable inquest.

"Well, tha's lost thi bike. Whatever 'es ta bin doin?" asked the father.

"Tryin' ter learn to ride," said the son, ruefully.

A householder had been buying horse manure for his roses from a small boy at £1 a bucketful. One week the price had risen to £2. "You see, mister," the boy explained, "mi brother pinched the sweeping brush, so this 'ere's 'and-picked."

A mother remarked to her small son: "Your hands are very clean today for a change. What has happened?"

"Oh, I've been practising whistling with my fingers," was the reply.

A small girl from up the dale recently visited some friends in town. She gazed long and earnestly at their well-filled bookshelves, and then declared: "We get books from the library van, too. But we have to return ours."

A Daleswoman lived in a village where the church was very old. It had 'box' pews, with a door at each end. One day, her little girl asked her: "When you go to church, mummy, which cupboard do you go in?"

At a village show on the North York Moors, there was a prize marrow well over two feet long and a foot in diameter.

Two local lads came up. The elder lad stroked the marrow nonchalantly and said to his friend: "Mi dad was going to bring ours, but we couldn't get it on t' truck."

A pupil in a West Riding school gave this definition of a Quaker: "A Quaker's a man 'at nivver grumles, nivver wants to feight an' nivver answers back. Mi father's a Quaker, mi mother is not."

After conducting the morning service at a village chapel, a Methodist local preacher arrived at the farm where he was being provided with dinner, a little earlier than anticipated. The farmer's wife told the little boy to take the preacher for a walk round the farm until dinner was ready. This pleased the lad and he was soon on friendly terms with the preacher.

In a burst of confidence he proudly said: "Ah know what sort of a pudding we are going to have for our dinner."

"Oh," exclaimed the preacher, "what sort is it going to be?"

"A jam roly-poly," said the lad.

"What makes you so sure," said the preacher.

"Well," replied the lad, "I noticed mi mother only 'ad one stocking on this morning."

A Dales farmer's wife remarked to her daughter: "I hope that's a nice book you're reading, dear."

"Oh, yes, Mum. It's a lovely book," said the small girl. "But I don't think you would like it. It's so sad at the end."

"In what way, dear?"

"Well," the small girl sighed. "She leaves him and he has to go back to his wife."

Harry told his granddad: "We gave a performance of *Hamlet* at school and a lot of fathers and mothers came. Although some of them had seen it before, they laughed just the same."

Two small boys were visiting their grandparents one Christmas and the younger one would persist in shouting up the chimney: "Santy Claus, Santy Claus, Ah want a motorcar."

"Give ower shaating," said his brother. "Santy Claus isn't deeaf."

"Ah knaw – bud mi grandfatther is."

Little Jean was watching her mother spread cream on her face.

"What's that for, mummy?" She asked.

"It's to make me beautiful, dear," replied her mother.

Jean watched her mother remove the cream, then in tones of great sadness whispered: "It didn't work, did it?"

One lovely feature of Yorkshire life was the custom of children calling at auntie's house about teatime, for a good tea was usually assured.

A boy following this custom found two other visitors were present. When time came 'to draw up to the table' the boy was invited to say grace.

"You know," said auntie, "like your mother does at home."

Each head was bowed and the grace came clearly: "For God's sake go easy on the butter."

"I'd take it back, mummy – it doesn't work."

"Nah, remember to do tha kerb drill," said the small boy instructing his smaller companion, "or," (rolling his eyes) "tha'll end up potted meeaht."

A small girl walked into the general shop in a Wharfedale village for her weekly purchase of sweets.

"Please may I have it in liquorice this week?" she said to the shopkeeper.

"I am afraid I have none, dear. Must it be liquorice?"

"Yes, please, I think it must," she replied. "You see my pet lamb has just died, and I'm in mourning."

In a back street the talk was between two five-year-old girls:

"Sylvia, have you got that chewing gum that I lent you?"

"No, I've lost it."

"Well, you'll have to find it, 'cos it's our Robert's."

At Hull Customs, a woman and her small daughter were having their baggage examined.

Suddenly, the small child, who had been watching the official, clapped her hands in great glee and called out loudly to her mother:

"He's getting warm now, isn't he mummy?"

One teatime a friend was unsuccessfully trying to coax her small son to eat some prunes. "God'll punish yer if yer doan't eit 'em," she said, but the little lad still refused.

"Reight," said mother, "yer goin straight to bed." She undressed the lad and put him to bed.

During the evening there was a terrific thunderstorm, and mother thought the lad would be scared; she went upstairs. He was pacing about the floor muttering:

"Thundering, leetnin', 'E's makin' a heck of a fuss over a few prunes."

Three-year-old Jane, on seeing snow falling for the first time, observed: "Come and look, Mam; it's raining rice pudding."

Recently a six-year-old grandson was being taken for his second visit to Knaresborough's Wishing Well. On the way he remarked to his grandfather: "It would save a lot of time if we went straight to the shop."

Fred once had a spell of door-to-door salesmanship and in his first inexperienced days called at one Dales house where a small boy opened the door to his knock.

"Is there no one else in?" Fred asked.

"Yes, my sister," said the boy brightly.

"Perhaps I could see her?" inquired Fred.

The boy disappeared and did not return for several minutes. Then his voice was heard calling: "You'd better come in. I can't lift her out of the play-pen."

A boy in a Dales village was asked by his pal to play out.

"Ah can't," he said, "Ah've got to stay in to help mi dad do mi homework."

A small boy was not impressed when a baby brother arrived at Christmas. When told it must have come from Santa Claus he complained: "Tommy next door got an electric railway and Sid's sister had a pony – and we've got this!"

WORK

farming – trouble at t' mill –
down the mines – road and rail

Let's face it, work is funny. It may not seem like it at the time when you're waiting for the bus to take you to the place that makes things out of plastic or you're taking a last gulp of fresh air before you plunge into the air-conditioned and hair-conditioned and fat-bloke-goateed world of the office. Take it from me, and from *Dalesman* gems in this chapter: it's funny.

My first job was working on the market in Barnsley. I didn't get a long-service medal or a clock because the job only lasted half an hour. I was taking a short cut through the market with my mate Chris Allatt on the way to the bus station sometime in 1967 in the summer before I went to the big school when a man in a cap shouted us: "Hey lads, do you want to earn a bit of belm?" I'd never heard the word belm before and I thought it was a meat product, like haslet or savoury duck; Chris was more worldy wise and he knew it meant money. We nodded and the man pointed to some carpets rolled up like giant cigars at the side of a stall. "If you can get them onto my van, I'll make it worth your while." Me and Chris spent hours and a couple of missed buses getting the carpets into the van and the bloke gave us a bob. Each, mind you. An old shilling. For all that work and sweat. I almost cried. Chris had more chutzpah: he chucked the bob high in the air where it turned and twisted and landed on an egg stall. On some eggs in the egg stall. Work is funny.

The second job I had was at my mate Martyn's dad's factory. I hung Stanley knives up all day long and Dick painted them. A lad worked there who I'd better not name because he reads the *Dalesman* and he might be getting this book for a Christmas present; he invariably arrived at work like a dropped cup: shattered. His eyelids drooped and it always felt like his next contribution to the debate would be a snore. One lunchtime he fell asleep, his mouth hanging open like Homer Simpson's, so we welded the steel toecaps of his boots to a girder. Work is funny, you see. Especially when Mr Fawcett banged a bucket with a spoon right next to the sleeping beauty's head and shouted that the factory was on fire.

The third job I had was at a building site near Sheffield. Let's pretend the firm was called Smith's. They found out I'd been to college and they put me in charge of the shed that they kept all the stores in. One night we got burgled and a load of doors got nicked. The coppers came and took statements but they told me they didn't hold out much hope of getting the goods back. Three nights later, in the small ads of the local evening paper, I noticed an advert: "Doors for sale. Just like Smith's." It's a fair cop!

So, in this chapter we'll encounter funny farmers and daft bankers, road sweepers who do silly things and comedy coppers. That the majority of the comedy is built around farming isn't unusual; much of the Dales is farming country, after all. And let me tell you confidentially that *Dalesman* is always looking for more funny farming anecdotes, particularly ones built round incomprehensible farming words. So, next time you're up in the Dales and you see a farmer leaning on a five-barred gate, approach him with a clipboard and ask him, since he's obviously got nothing to do, to tell you something funny. I guarantee a response.

Work is funny: always remember that.

Ian McMillan

During the depression between the two wars, a lad got so tired of being on the 'dole' that he decided to ask a fell sheep farmer for a job.

"Does tha think tha can help wi' t' sheep?"

"Aye, Ah can manage owt."

"Well, now, Ah'll gi' thi a trial. Go up t' moor an' bring in t' sheep – all on 'em."

After an hour or two the farmer went down to the fold to see what had happened. There were the sheep all safely gathered in, but the youth was lying on his back – he was absolutely 'flat out'.

"By gow," said the farmer, as he looked into the fold, "tha's done a grand job. But hey. What's that tha's getten? Why, man alive, theer's a fox among 'em."

"Is there?" wearily replied the lad. "Well, he's geed me more trouble than all t' rest put together."

A farmer was watching his man manuring 'taty rows'. "Put plenty in," he said, "taties are hungry things."

The man replied. "Ah noticed that at dinner-time in that meat and taty pie we had. In that piece I got, taties had etten all t' meat."

During a conversation in a North Yorkshire pub, a middle-aged farmer told a visitor that his father, ninety years old, was still on the farm where he was born.

"Ninety years old?" commented the visitor.

"Yes, Dad is that."

"Is his health good?"

"T'aint much now. He's been complainin' for a few months back."

"What's the matter with him?"

"I dunno; sometimes I think farmin' don't agree with him."

It was in the days when water had to be pumped and carried to the stock by bucket.

The farm lad was told to water the cow, and when sometime later he was asked if he had finished he answered with not a little disgust:

"The aud devil supped twelve buckets, so Ah threw t' last three ovver 'er; noo she's wet outside as well as in."

A rather short-tempered farmer had a somewhat unsatisfactory sheepdog. One day when holding open a gate for the flock to be driven through he got so vexed with the poor dog that he shouted:

" 'Ere, cum and hod' yat open and Ah'll drive t' b----rs through missen."

A young lady on holiday in Swaledale thought she would like to work on a farm, so she called on a local farmer and asked if she could help him with his sheep.

"Ah want a shepherd for my sheep, not a shepherdess," he said.

"But surely there's no reason why a woman shouldn't do the job as well as a man," said the girl.

"Oh yes there is. A woman once tried it and made a mess of it."

"Who was she?"

"Bo Peep."

Two Dales farmers were sitting in the snug of the local inn. They both had many acres of hay lying sodden in the fields, and the rain still fell as it had done for the past four days. After being glumly silent for half an hour, one of them heaved a long-drawn-out sigh. The other, after contemplating his friend with a look of sympathy, remarked: "You're telling me."

"This pig's ticking."
"Aye, that's t' one that swallowed my watch."

Yorkshire farmer, knocking hard on bedroom door of hired hand, very early in the morning: "Cum on, lad, it's time tha wer' up."

Voice from within (very muffled): "What time is it?"

Farmer: "Half past fower."

Voice: "Is it raining?"

Farmer: "No, it isn't."

Voice: "Is it snawing?"

Farmer: "Naw."

Voice: "Is it foggy?"

Farmer, now getting very rattled: "Naw, it isn't."

Voice: "Aw, well, is it Sunday?"

Farmer (after an abrupt silence): "Naw, it isn't Sunday."

Voice, rather triumphantly: "Well then, I'm badly."

A Wensleydale farm lad bought a watch for five shillings which was guaranteed to remain in good order for five years. At the end of the first year the lad took the watch back to the shop and announced that it wouldn't go.

"Nah then, lad, tha's 'ad an accident wi' it, hasn't ta?" queried the watchmaker.

"Aye that's reight, mister. Ah did 'ave a bit o' a' accident," the lad replied. "Tha sees, six months sin' Ah were feeding t' pigs and t' watch fell into t' trough."

"Six months sin'," said the watchmaker. "Thou owt t' browt it back afore now."

"Ah couldn't," said the lad. "We nobbut killed t' owd pig yesterday."

The farmer had just hired a lad.

"An' what shall Ah hev ta do?" said the boy.

The farmer looked him up and down.

"Do?" he answered. "Do? Tha'll hev ta wark. Ah can laik bi misen."

A young farm lad was given the task of counting some moor lambs through a hole in a wall. Sometimes they went rather quickly and the lad got a bit mixed, but he kept on counting. When they had all passed through he took them into a turnip field where the farmer was busy setting a net.

"Hoo monny hez tha?" the farmer asked.

"Whya," said the lad, "Ah gat a bit muddled. There's either eighty-six or eighty-seven."

"Thoo's gitten t' lot, then," said his boss. "There's nobbut eighty-farve when ther all theer."

An old Yorkshire farmer was continually being pestered to take out a policy by an insurance man. Again and again he called, but each time the farmer sent him away, saying he could find "summat else to do wi' me brass".

One day, however, the farmer's barn caught fire, and in the midst of the excitement the farmer was seen charging down the village street, shouting: "Wheer's that insurance chap? 'E's nivver 'ere when 'E's wanted."

John had worked for nearly sixty years on a Yorkshire farm. One day his employer ventured gently to suggest that it was time he retired. The old man was indignant.

"Soa it's cummed ti this, 'as it?" he asked. "Ah'm not want-ed neer longer? Ah worked for thi grandfather, an' for thi father, an' Ah tell thi, if Ah'd known this here job warn't going to be permanent, Ah'd nivver 'ave taken it on."

Up in Swaledale some years ago there lived an old chap who went round doing jobs for farmers, for which he was reward-ed by small sums of money or something off the farm.

One December he reminded one farmer: "Ah thowt ye said ye were goin' to go to gie me a turkey for Christmas?"

"Aye," said the farmer. " 'Appen Ah did, but it got better."

A local farmer of the old horse and cart days was given to growling about one crop or another. If it was commented that his wheat had done well, for instance, he would immediately declare that he had had no luck with his potatoes. But one year every prospect seemed to please.

"Bumper crops all round," commented one of the farmer's friends.

"Aye," growled back the farmer, "an' it damned nearly killed t' osses bringin' t' stuff in."

An East Riding farmer was teaching two trainee ploughmen to plough a straight furrow.

"Fix your eye on something at the other end of the field," he said.

Sam's furrow was straight as a die, but Dick's was very crooked.

"What did you fix your eye on?" Dick asked Sam.

"The tree yonder," answered Sam.

"Oh, that accounts for it," said Dick. "I fixed my eye on that white cow, and she went grazing all over t' place."

A Wolds farmer devised a marvellous scarecrow. It waved its arms in the breeze. It had an alarming tin rattle that went off at intervals. And it carried a dummy gun.

He was asked if it really scared the birds after all his effort.

"Noo, Ah reckons it does. Why, only the other day them crows brought back some corn they had stole from me two years ago."

After working alongside his men one Monday, a Dales farmer did not seem happy with the results of the day's labour.

Turning to them he said: "Just think on, a day and an arf after tomorrer the biggest arf o' the week will a gone, an' nowt done."

An old Yorkhire farmer amused his friends at the 'local'. It all started when someone asked him how his hens were laying.

"They've all stopped, every one of them," he replied.

"Can you account for it?" asked the landlord.

"I believe I can," the farmer said. "It's like this. I've been having a small shippon built and the bricklayers have been on piece-work. I'll swear my hens were listening when them chaps were swanking about the wages they earn laying bricks."

Two men working on a Dales farm were moving chicken coops when to their horror, a rat ran from under one, and disappeared up the trouser leg of the younger man.

Petrified, he clasped his hands round the top of his leg and yelled: "Quick, do summat."

"It's alreight lad," came the comforting reply. "Thee just 'old it theer while Ah fotch mi gun."

A Dales butcher's lad was riding his carrier bicycle very fast down the village street and he crashed at the bottom of the hill, sprawling across his machine and basket.

Passing villagers gave assistance. On being asked if he was all right, the butcher's lad replied: "Ah'm all reight – but Ah've lost me heart, me liver's mucky and one of me kidneys has rolled down that drain."

One day, as the stationmaster was collecting tickets at the gateway, a dog jumped out of the guard's van and dashed away through the crowd of travellers into the road.

Shouting at the top of his voice, he said: "Hey! Stop that dog, stop that dog – it's a parcel."

Tommy was not impressed with the arrogance of the new mill foreman: "The less a chap knows, the prouder he is of his knowledge."

"Stop! Parcel!"

31

There was a Yorkshire character in years gone by who was in great demand at spreading time. He earned his money by odd jobs, and one day a farmer asked him if he would help on the farm. Just before he was due to arrive from muck-spreading this farmer met a friend at the auction mart.

"If you're hiring old John, I've a tip for you," said the friend. "Decide how much he can reasonably do in a day, and then put a few acres on top of your reckoning. Say 'you'll only be able to do this stretch today; the rest will do until tomorrow.' Then watch John work. He'll do the lot if he's to work all night. John doesn't like folk to think he's not capable."

"Are tha on strike ageean?"
"Aye."
"What's it for this time?"
"Ah doan't rightly know – but we shall get it."

An accountant was assisting a not-so-young Dales farmer with this work. He read out the questions and the farmer client provided the requisite answers.

Eventually he came to that classic question, which must have been designed specially for Dales businesses: "Will your records be kept on a computer?"

The farmer replied: "My records'll be kept on t' same spike they've allus bin kept on."

The new farmhand certainly had a hearty appetite as he sat down to his first meal with the family.

"Thank you, missus, that was very tasty," he said to the farmer's wife as he finished.

"You've only eaten four platefuls," she replied sarcastically. "I was beginnin' to think you weren't keen on my cooking."

"Well, you know, it doesn't pay to eat too much on an empty stomach, like."

Some years ago when motoring signs were appearing as a rash on the Yorkshire countryside, an East Yorkshire farmer watched as workmen erected a 30mph sign on the outskirts of his village. Eventually he approached one of the workmen and asked what it meant.

"It means you've got to go thirty miles an hour through the village," he was told.

The farmer removed his hat and scratched his head. Finally, he said: "C'm up, Dobbin, I doubt if ye've got it in ye, but we'll 'ev a try."

A new lad was taken on at a mill where they were working overtime, and so they told him to bring three meals – breakfast, dinner and tea – with him when he came in the morning.

The next day when he knocked off for breakfast he undid his red handkerchief and saw three teacakes, each one cut in two to make a sandwich. He opened one of them and found there was nothing inside except butter. Then he opened the next one, and that was the same. And so was the third.

"Why, here's a fine carry-on," roared the lad. "Ha the heck am Ah ta tell which o' these is me breakfast?"

A man on the outskirts of Leeds employed an old countryman – who lived by doing odd jobs – to dig over his garden. After some time he went to see how the work was progressing. The odd job man was making valiant efforts at digging, but was handicapped by a voluminous overcoat which trailed about his arms and feet. His temporary employer suggested that the man might find the work easier and make more progress if he removed the overcoat.

"Nay," said the odd job man. "Ah've got three prices. One and ninepence an hour wi' me overcoit on. Two shillings an hour wi' me overcoit off. And two and thrupence an hour wi' me coit off as well. Tha's nobbut paying one and ninepence."

"There's a good dog!"

Bill approached the foreman: "Onny chance of a job?" he enquired.

Foreman: "Can ter dew owt wi' a shuvvel?"

Bill: "Ah can fry some 'am on it."

Foreman: "Well, for thi' cheek, lad, Ah'll set thee on. Away wi' thee an' 'elp yon chap ter loading t' motor-wagon."

Shortly afterwards the foreman tapped the new hand on the shoulder.

"Ah say, lad," he says, "doesta know that chap's throwin' two shuvvels-full ter thee one?"

Bill: "Aye, Ah do, but Ah've telled 'im abaht it."

The foreman asked a limping man what had happened: "Hurt yourself, Fred?"

Fred: "Nay, I've gotten a nail sticking up in mi' boot."

Foreman: "Then why don't you take it out?"

Fred: "What, in mi' dinner hour?"

The chief constable of a small Yorkshire town was also an expert veterinary surgeon. One night the telephone rang. The chief constable's wife answered it.

"Is Mr Blank there?" said an agitated voice.

"Do you want my husband in his capacity of veterinary surgeon or as a chief constable?" inquired the woman.

"Both, madam," came the reply. "We can't get our bulldog to oppen 'is mouth – and there's a burglar in it."

A sailor on his way out of Hull docks approached a policeman and said confidentially: "Will it be all right if I bring out some tobacco tomorrow? I'll make it all right with you."

"Right-ho," replied the cop. But the next day when he saw the sailor he stopped him and had him searched.

"Thought better of it, eh?" he chuckled on finding nothing.

"Oh, no," replied the sailor. "I brought it out yesterday."

A Yorkshireman was walking down the street when he passed a horse pulling a coal cart. He was amazed when the horse spoke, saying "Hello, Bob." It was unmistakably his old friend Bill who had returned to life as a horse.

"Well, how do you like the work, Bill?"

"Oh, it's tough going," he said, "pulling along these roads. I'm bullied and have no rest."

"Well, you can speak, why don't you tell the coalman?" asked Bob.

"Oh, I daren't do that. He'll have me shouting 'coal' next."

A youth who did odd jobs for the local blacksmith in a small Yorkshire town, was given an old watch by his employer.

One day Abe arrived at the smithy and announced sadly. "T' watch 'as stopped."

"Then we'd better 'ave a look at it, lad," said the blacksmith, removing the back of the watch.

Inside was a small dead fly.

Abe's eyes widened.

"Ee, noa wonder it's stopped," he said slowly, "t' driver's deead."

A building site foreman who phoned his boss for more shovels got the reply: "Got no more I'm afraid; men will have to lean on one another."

Alf and Joe were two Yorkshire street sweepers who had for long been at daggers drawn. Each was certain in his own mind that he was the better man at his job. One day they met and Alf started chipping Joe about his abilities.

Joe replied: "I'm t' best sweeper in t' town, Ah tell thee."

"Sweeper?" answered Alf. "Tha's all reight when tha's sweepin' muck straight down t' gutter, but when tha' comes to a bit o' 'scientific work' round a lamp-post, tha'rt licked."

Many years ago there lived at Malton a coal dealer who was 'a bit of a character'.

One day as he was doing his rounds his horse fell down dead. Scratching his head the coal merchant remarked: "Well, Ah've nivver known him do that before."

One morning on his way to the train station, Abe noticed that his pocket watch was missing, so as he passed the police station he reported its loss.

"We will leave no stone unturned to find it," they told him, and Abe went away satisfied.

That night Abe arrived back at the station to find workmen digging up the street (they were preparing to lay the tramlines). Rushing to the police station, he exclaimed: "Don't rive up any more setts. Ah've found t' watch in mi other pocket. Ah'm just sorry to 'ave put yer to soa much trouble."

An old *Dalesman* once offered this advice about selecting a man to work in the garden:

"Tha mun goa by 'is trousis. If they're patched on t' knees, you want 'im; if they're patched on t' seat, you don't."

A joiner examined a window frame his apprentice was making.

"Nay, me lad," he exclaimed in disgust. "I nivver saw sic a winda frame."

"Oh," the boy replied, "but I hev."

"Nivver," said his master emphatically. The lad drew his previous effort from under his bench, saying: "Then what d'yer think o'that?"

A lorry driver was sitting in a service station café on the A1 motorway. Another driver approached him and said:

"Hullo, Jim. What you got there – tea or coffee?"

"Nay," replied Jim sadly. "They didn't say."

A man in West Yorkshire called in the local property repairer to attend to a leaking roof. The man was taken into an upstairs room and shown where the missing slate was. An hour or so later the man appeared to be packing up his tools so he was asked if he had replaced the missing slate.

His reply was: "Well, no – you see, I can tell now where the water is coming in, but if I replace that slate I shan't know where the leak is."

Having reached the age of sixty, Joe, a Huddersfield weaver, could no longer see to do his work, and his wife was greatly distressed at this state of affairs. Then one day he came home and said: "Buck up, lass, Ah've getten a job as a neet watchman."

His wife burst into tears. "Well, if that isn't t' limit," she sobbed, "just when Ah've made thee two new neet-shirts."

A tea-time bus wound its way slowly down the remoter part of a well-known dale. The driver knew almost every passenger and where to collect the odd parcel. He even paused to allow a late customer from a farm off the roadside to catch the bus.

At a certain lane end, the bus was stopped, engine ticking over, for a long time. The driver looked agitatedly at his watch.

"Ivv'ry day for a fortneet," he said, shaking his head. "Ivv'ry day for a fortneet."

A minute ticked past. The driver reached for his gear lever. Suddenly a small middle-aged figure appeared from a farmhouse down the lane and hurried towards the bus. To everyone's surprise, the driver slipped the gear in, and the bus jolted down the road.

"It's four 'ours to t' next bus," he said, turning towards the rest of the passengers: then, with that slight relaxation of the facial muscle that passes for a grin in the West Riding, added: " 'Appen she'll be on time termorrer."

There is a carpenter in a certain Dales village whose work leaves much to be desired.

It was not very long ago that a newcomer to the village wanted a new wheelbarrow and so he inquired of a local resident whether he thought the carpenter could make him a good one.

The local resident scratched his head thoughtfully before he replied. "Aye, 'appen he'll be able to make yer a wheelbarrow. But Ah reckon that if it runs as well as his water butts, it'll be a good 'un."

The telephone officer was on duty at a West Riding fire station, and when he took a call, heard a woman's timid voice.

"Is that the fire station?" she asked.

"Yes, that's right," replied the fireman eagerly.

"Well," continued the voice, "I've just had a new rock garden built, and I've put in some plants, but…"

"Where's the fire?" the fireman yelled.

"Some of these plants are very expensive, and…" the voice went on.

"Look here," the officer broke in, "what you want is a flower shop."

"No, I don't," said the voice. "I'm coming to that in a minute. My neighbour's house is on fire, and I don't want you firemen tramping over my garden when you come here."

Bill was mending the driving belt in the spinning shed, and Joe, a young apprentice, was helping.

Suddenly the engine started and Bill was taken round a couple of times, with Joe gaping.

Then Bill was thrown off, and Joe ran to him, crying: "Eh, arter hurt, arter dead? Spake to ma, Bill."

Bill said: "Will I hell us spake to thee. I've passed thee twice, and tha' niver let on."

At a Dentdale sawmill, Joe and Ned were 'throng' making a waterwheel. The day wore on. Joe thought longingly of catching the early bus home – to tea and slippers.

"Let's gi' owwer, Ned," he burst out at last. "Rome wasn't built in a day."

But Ned had other ideas. "Neea, it wasn't," he replied. "I wasn't foreman."

Sam is quite a character and lives in a Yorkshire mining village. One day, instead of the usual water, he took to work a bottle of the sparkling mineral variety. He was late coming into the 'gate' where the men had their 'snap' and on arrival he discovered that his bottle of water had gone.

He spoke no word, but went back to the face, returning with a large coal hammer. He walked back and forth in front of his workmates, swinging the hammer, and maintaining an ominous silence.

At last one of the men said: "What's up, Sam? What are ta' walkin' abaat like that for?"

"Ah'm waitin' for t' first un that belches," retorted Sam.

Three small boys were discussing their fathers' work.

Said one: "My dad makes model ships and he gets £10 for every one he makes."

"My dad writes for the papers and he gets paid for every line he writes," said another.

"Nay, that's nowt," said the third. "My father's a minister. He preaches for half an hour and it takes two men to collect the money for him."

REST AND PLAY

church and chapel – days out and holidays –
sport – music – food and drink

If work is funny, and we proved it was in the previous chapter, then play is funnier. And, let's face it, Yorkshire people
are built for pleasure. Look at our broad shoulders from years
of carrying foaming pints on heavy trays; look at the crows'
feet around our eyes which isn't just caused by the wind coming in from the North Sea but by the constant laughing we
indulge in all the way across the three Ridings when people
fall down or tell us something funny or make a daft noise with
any part of their body. Look at our mouths, ready to tell a joke
or crack a smile or laugh until our socks fly off like starlings.

So in this section of the book you'll be in the company of
pub football teams whose method of training is to just have
one bag of crisps rather than two. A family bag, mind you.
You'll be in the company of funny uncles who do such bad
impressions at the drop of a hat that you're always careful not
to drop any hats. You'll be in the company of families who go
to Scarborough on their holidays and the landlady in the B&B
charges them for the bathplug, and you'll be in the company
of people who, whatever terrible and depressing things happen, still come up smiling because they're from Yorkshire.

This section of the book is also the holy section, so you'll
meet jolly vicars and people who suck breezeblock-sized mints
in sermons and people who won't go out on a Sunday without a hat that looks, to quote the great thriller writer Raymond
Chandler, like it's been taken from its mother too young.

There was a Primitive Methodist chapel not far from our house and I asked my mother what Primitive Methodists did. "They swing across the chapel on a rope," she replied, dead-pan. I believed her till last week. My Uncle Charlie had his own version of the Lord's Prayer that began "Harp lager, till half eleven, alehead be thy name…"

In this section you'll also find brass bands and pigeon fly-ing, and the kinds of things that people often do to keep them-selves occupied: not both at the same time, obviously. That would be daft.

Ian McMillan

A vicar was staying at a farm in the Dales and on Sunday evening told the three children the story of the Prodigal Son. He described the welcome prepared by the father, how he killed the fatted calf, and bade his servants invite the neigh-bours in so that they could all eat, drink, and be merry.

"And who do you think it was," he asked them, "who was sorry that the Prodigal Son had come home?"

"Of course we know who it was," said the youngest child promptly. "It was that poor dear little fatted calf."

A Daleswoman said she had had a 'locust preacher' staying at her home one Sunday. "Nay, Sarah," said her friend. "Tha's got-ten t' wrong word. It's a 'local' preacher, not 'locust'. Locusts is them creatures what eyt up everything i' front of 'em."

"Why then, it's same thing," said Sarah. "For yon chap eyt up everything Ah set afore 'im all right."

Young Johnnie had the misfortune to swallow a shilling.

"Send for the doctor," said his mother.

"Nay, we'll send for the vicar," said his father. "He's the best one round here for getting money out of folks."

"Uh oh, we're in trouble – t' Prodigal Son's back."

A local preacher arrived home from an appointment and was asked by his wife how he had gone on.

"Grand in t' afternoon," he said, "but at neet Ah'd only a varry poor time."

"How's that?"

"Ah wor entertained to tea at a farm. They gave me a good helping o'goose, an' just after t' service 'ed started it must have wanted to flap its wings."

"Is your new parson any good?"

"Nay. Ah reckon nowt to him. It taks him forty minutes to put us to sleep. T' owd 'un did it in fifteen."

A certain Wensleydale cleric who was accomplished at spinning a natural bait over a trout made a practice, it is said, of keeping his supply of minnows alive in the church. His secret was revealed when a heated argument developed between the sexton and a proud mother desirous of a mid-week christening. She had invited her friends and made a special baking for the great event.

"Wednesday's out o' all reckoning," said the exasperated official. "Parson has t' font full o' live minnows and he's nut garn fishing til Thursday."

A Methodist minister was conducting a baptismal service, the father of the child being a local working man.

On being asked to name the child the minister was astounded to hear 'Homer', for he had not suspected that this member of his flock was a classical scholar.

At the conclusion of the service he said to the father: "I had no idea you were interested in the classics." The father looked blank so the minister enquired about his choice of Homer as a name for his son.

To which the father replied: "You see, I keep pigeons."

A visiting preacher to a country church, on meeting the verger, said: "Please will you make sure there is a glass of water in the pulpit?"

"Oh aye," said the verger, "there is some there. I filled glass up last Sunday and t' parson nobbut supped aaf on it."

Mr Jones had recently become father of triplets. The minister stopped him in the street to congratulate him.

"Well, Mr Jones," he said, "I hear that the Lord has smiled on you."

"Smiled on me," repeated Jones. "He laughed out loud."

The parson met one of his flock in a North Yorkshire village street and stopped to speak to him.

"John, my good man," he said severely, "your wife tells me that your conduct of late has not been at all desirable. Why don't you take a lesson from me? I can go to the village and come back again without getting drunk."

"Aye, mebbe you can, sir," replied the other, "but, you see, I'm popular."

A Methodist lay preacher used to boast about how much he got at the collection. One Sunday he was preaching at the local chapel, which was full to bursting, but as he was going up the pulpit steps he noticed that a group from the neighbouring – and more prosperous – village was trying to get in the door. "Na then," he cried out. "Make way everyone, and let t' half-crowners come forrard."

A local preacher who conducted a service at a small Dales chapel where the congregation numbered only two was told by the chapel-keeper-cum-organist as she made her way to the organ: "Cut thy sermon short when tha smells t' Yorksher pudding."

"Don't look back or you'll turn to salt!"

The doctor asked the farmer's wife: "Did you give your husband the sleeping powder as prescribed?"

"Yes," she replied. "You said I had to give him enough to cover a three-penny piece. I didn't have one, so I used three pennies. But it's all reight, he's still sleeping."

An elderly farmer had for some time been having treatment for his rheumatics, which was very effective. A friend said to him: "Well, Ah reckon tha's fair set up wi' theesen noo these getten rid o' t' rheumatics."

"Nay, Ah doan't know so much," was the reply. "Tha see's Ah carn't tell noo when it's gahn ti rain."

The Nonconformist preacher was getting a little carried away in his sermon:

"Why, Keighley and Bingley are no better than...than Sodom and Gomorrah...on a smaller scale, of course."

The manager of a Leeds music hall was testing the abilities of a few candidates for stage honours, and this is how he let down one of the would-be funny men:

"Your songs won't do for me. I can't allow any profanity in my theatre."

"But I don't use profanity," was the reply.

"No," replied the manager, "but the audience would."

Old George had trouble with his leg. He went to the surgery about it. As he wrote out a prescription, the doctor said: "Let me see, George, how old are you?"

"Eighty-fower," replied George.

"Well, now," said the doctor, "I think, don't you, that we can put this bad leg of yours down to old age?"

"Nowt o' t' sort," said George, indignantly. "T' other leg's same age an' there's nowt wrong wi' that."

An East Riding optician was testing a farm lad's eyesight. He hung a test card on the wall and asked him to read the line which ran: S P T Z F K Y L.

The lad screwed up his face and stared at the letters until the optician said impatiently: "Come, now, surely you can read those big letters."

"Aye," said the lad. "Hoo can read 'em all reet, but hoo can't pronounce the word."

Before one choir rehearsal the relative merits of local ladies were being discussed, and of course their voices. From the back came: "Clara has a fine range." Pause for this to sink in, then: "But she can't cook."

A male voice choir competed yearly at Blackpool, and made the occasion a full day's outing. Arriving by the sea they enjoyed a paddle. This was the routine for several years, and then one year it was noticed that one of the baritones had very black legs. He was chaffed. "By gum, Bill, thi' legs is mucky!" Bill replied: "Well, yer mun remember, Ah cudn't cum last year."

Some years ago a musical concert was to be held at Runswick Bay and the task of organising it had been left to a somewhat unmusical lady. She made a list in order of the different items of the concert such as 'choir', 'duet', 'solo', etc.

However, when the chairman read through the programme he suddenly noticed one item headed: 'O, O, O'. He asked the organiser whatever 'O, O, O' was supposed to mean.

The lady turned round and indignantly replied: "Don't be daft, that means trio."

A vicar's comments about the new organist: "We've had some bad organists in this church. Some couldn't read music – but he's so bad he can't read the words."

"Did you give your husband the mustard plaster I ordered?"

"Yes, doctor, but he says, could he have a bit o' bread or something with the next one – it was terribly hot eating it on its own."

A concert had been arranged by the workers at a mill in Huddersfield, and all the local stars were booked to appear.

Miss Handloom, the favourite soprano, was announced. Before she began she apologised for her cold. Then she started.

"I'll hang my harp on a weeping willow-tree-e-e-ahem."

"On a weeping willow-tree-e-e-oh."

Her voice broke on the high note each time. She tried another two times.

A voice came from the back of the hall: "Try hangin' it on a lower branch, lass."

It was the local band concert.

"What's the next piece, Jim?" asked the trombone player.

"Handel's *Largo*," said Jim.

"Bah gum!" exclaimed the trombonist. "I've only just played that."

The choir were rehearsing an oratorio under their enthusiastic choirmaster who 'lived' for music. He stopped them with an anguished cry: "No, no, no; stop; stop, stop. Ah've told yer afoor – it's sopranos on their own till yer come to t' gates o' Hell, then yer *all* come in."

Some years ago a conductor of a village band in the East Riding at one rehearsal had occasion to reprove a player.

"Mr Smith," he said, "you are two bars behind the others."

From the player came the testy reply:

"Aye, Ah know. But you needn't bother about that. I can catch 'em up any time I want to."

During a concert in the village hall the new secretary was at the door taking the money. Just before the concert started he went off to find the caretaker.

When he found him he whispered: "If I were you I'd go careful or you'll be having trouble."

"Why, what's trouble?" demanded the caretaker.

"It's bigamy, that's what it is. I've just let in two women free who said they were the caretaker's wife. And now there's a third wanting to come in."

Father had returned home early from the village dance – at midnight. His daughter came in about 1am. Mother returned a few minutes later and was about to lock up when the daughter called out: "Don't lock the door mother – grandma isn't in yet."

The final session of a Dales musical competition was drawing to a close when the secretary, perturbed at the non-arrival of a number of the trophies, approached the chairman and informed him of the predicament.

Summoning his chauffeur, the chairman gave him instructions to drive home and ask the butler to give him half-a-dozen cups 'off the sideboard'. The cups were duly delivered and the presentation of prizes went according to programme.

The conductor of the winning band was handed a beautiful trophy; another was presented to the winning tenor. When the leading soprano received her cup, however, she glanced at the inscription and fell in a faint. The inscription read: 'Open competition for the best pig in the show'.

"Looks like a bad storm coming up," said the Dales hostess. "You'd better stay for dinner."

"Oh thanks," said the guest absently, "but I don't think it will be that bad."

"And where's tha been till this time?!"

Near Scarborough, some years ago, a youthful group went round the village singing Christmas carols joined by three of the local brass band.

Their joint effort was rather bad. The brass trumpet sounded out of tune. This was tactfully remarked upon and the musician replied: "Blow it, Ah's gotten trombone music."

Some years ago in the refreshment room at the old Midland station at Leeds, a middle-aged woman struggled with a hot cup of coffee, trying to gulp it down before train time and keeping an eye on the clock as she did.

An old farmer fellow nearby saw her plight and called out: "Here, missus, tak my cup o' coffee. It's already saucered and blowed."

The annual meeting of the brass band was being held many years ago, under the chairmanship of a local councillor. Things had not been going very well during the year and the chairman announced that the expected balance sheet was nom de plume.

A local reporter whispered: "Non est." Whereupon the chairman replied: "Whether it's non est or nom de plume, we haven't got one."

It was the local operatic society's presentation of an American musical. During one romantic scene, coloured pieces of paper were seen to be floating from the ceiling – hesitantly at first, but later in profusion.

One voluble Yorkshireman was obviously bewildered by this. All was explained by the words of the song, but not, apparently, to his satisfaction.

"What's that falling?" he enquired of his neighbour.

"Blossoms," was the laconic reply.

"Ah'm reight glad. Ah thought it were whitewash."

One lovely summer in the 1950s, Tom took his father out to lunch at a very large hotel. The following day he was telling his mother how nice it had been.

"What did you have?" she asked.

"Oh, you know, the usual: Sunday roast beef and Yorkshire pudding."

Father exclaimed: "Yorkshire pudding? I never had any."

"Oh, you had," Tom replied.

Then the penny dropped. "Well," he said disgustedly, "that puffed-up thing; I thought it were a bread bun. I were in two minds whether to eat it with my knife and fork or pick it up in my fingers. By gum, I'll have mother off to teach 'em how to make a real Yorkshire pudding."

The village cricket match was in progress, being umpired by the local farmer. His son, a competent batsman, had been at the wicket from 2.30 to 5 o'clock when Dad gave him out after an lbw appeal.

At supper, the son said: "I don't think that was out, Dad."

"No lad, it wasn't – but them cows wanted milkin'."

Mary visited a friend, and for tea they had a home-made dish known as savoury duck, a kind of black pudding. Mary ate it with relish, and complimented her friend upon it.

"Ay, 'twere varry good," commented her friend, "but there'd o' bin more liver in it if t' cat 'adn't hev had a chaw at it while me back wor turned."

"I was thinking of going to a cricket match today," said one man to another, "but you know how it is – trying to find a place to park, getting through the crowd to get in, and besides, if it doesn't rain, it may be terribly hot."

"Yes, I know what you mean," replied his friend. "My wife won't let me go either."

An old Ryedale farmer had never been to York although he always wanted to see the city, so he went for the day and had a pleasant few hours looking round. Then he went to a restaurant for a meal. He began with chicken soup.

He looked puzzled when he tasted it. "What do they call this?" he asked.

"Chicken soup," the waiter replied.

"Nay," he commented. "That chicken must've walked through this soup on stilts."

One of the local lads was batting for his cricket team. When the ball came he would swipe at it, but in almost every case miss it.

One of the older members of the village who was watching said to another: "Fred isn't doing much today."

"Neer," said his pal. "Ah think he'd be better mowin' t' nettles."

A cricketer appealed for lbw. As there was no answer, he turned round to the umpire. There he was standing up, yet asleep. When he had wakened him he shouted: "I'm appealing for leg before."

"Did it hit yer leg, Jamie?" asked the umpire.

"Aye," said Jamie.

"Then yer'r oot, Jamie," said the umpire sadly.

Some years ago a village cricket match took place in which an opposition batsman was given 'out' by the home team umpire on a decision that appeared to the batsman as wrong. On passing the umpire on his way to the pavilion, the batsman, by that time in a subdued rage, said to the umpire:

"Y' doan't know t' first darned thing about umpiring."

To which the umpire replied: "Aye, and thoo doesn't know t' first thing about batting, else thoo wouldn't 'ave been out."

During a Dales cricket match one of the opening batsman snicked the ball into the stumper's hands. Upon appealing, the umpire gave the decision "Not out."

In the same over the batsman, an honest fellow whose conscience troubled him, got to the other end and said to the umpire: "Tha knaws Ah 'it that ball."

"Ah knaw tha did," responded that worthy, "but it wor nobbut slight."

A village team was playing cricket in an away match at the neighbouring village.

In the first four balls, 'their' umpire disallowed two lbw appeals by the opening fast bowler, who was also the captain. Hitching his trousers for the task ahead, he bellowed out in a voice which could be heard back in his own village: "Right lads, we'll get nowt there – we'll just have to bowl this lot out."

At a village cricket match the squire was given out lbw. He stopped on his way to the pavilion and spoke to the man in the white coat. "You really need glasses my man, giving me out like that."

"So do you," came the reply. "I'm selling ice-cream."

The umpire in the Bradford League was having trouble with a bowler. His persistent appeals for lbw decisions were too frequent and the umpire was annoyed. After again turning down a vociferous appeal, he said to the bowler: "Sitha, lad – thee get on wi' thi laiking; I'll tell tha when he's out."

On a bus en route to the Scarborough Cricket Festival, when he asked the conductor for a ticket to the cricket ground, the gentleman seated next to him said: "That's where I'd be going if I could get shut of the wife. All my married life I've been trying to interest her in cricket. But she won't be here for ever."

A Yorkshire rugby league match between two rival teams had reached a critical stage, with the scores equal and each side trying ferociously to gain an advantage.

Several players had already been carried off and several more had their jerseys ripped when a particularly strong kick by one of the full-backs sent the ball right out of the ground.

The players hesitated, wondering what was to happen next. They were spurred on by a voice from the crowd: "Never mind t' ball, lads, get on with t' game."

The Yorkshireman, now living in the South, bought himself a bag of golf clubs, presented himself to the professional and said: "Nah then." The professional told him that all he had to do was to take his club and hit his ball on to the green away in the distance.

The Yorkshireman spat on his hands and hit the ball with a terrific wallop. It sailed away to land fairly in the centre of the green.

"That right?" he asked, and the professional assured him it was a good stroke. They went on to the green and the Yorkshireman said: "Well, what do I do next?"

"Well, you hit it into this little hole," said the professional.

"Well, what the heck," roared the Yorkshireman. "Why couldn't tha tell me that afore I hit it t' first time?"

Two local football teams had been engaged in fierce combat for over half an hour when one of the visiting side was seen to limp off the field.

Immediately the home captain sent one of his men off.

"You're a real sport," remarked an admirer at the interval. "I suppose you don't like the idea of playing eleven men against ten, eh?"

"No, it's not that," replied the other, "but our chaps have left their money in the dressing room."

A Dales farmer was in Leeds one weekend and a friend took him to a rugby league match, the farmer never having seen the game before.

Back in the village local he was asked: "What is this rugby league like, John, lad?"

To which John replied: "It's queerest game ye iver saw. A lot of strapping chaps wi' pants at arn't long enough for 'em, were chasing abart after a bit of a ball and throwing it to one another.

"Then one on 'em got this ball and streaked for a white line. He fell on this ball ower this line and three of four on 'em fell on him. T' crowd all shouted 'Try, Try'.

"But tha knaws, try as they would they couldn't burst it."

He was playing in a football match and headed a goal. As he returned to his position on the wing, highly delighted at his success, he overheard the following comment from a spectator: "Tha didn't scower that. Yon ball 'it thee."

On a cold winter's day, John and Albert were maggot fishing at Linton. As the outing drew to a close, Albert struck smartly but without reward.

"You didn't have a bite," commented John.

"Mi float dothered."

"Well if it did, it wor nobbut thi maggots shivering because they're feeling t' cold so much."

"Well," said the chairman of the parish council. "You can talk all night about this chandelier for the parish 'all, but I'm going to tell 'e what I thinks of it.

"There be three reasons why we shouldn't waste our money on such fripperies. First, there's none of us can spell chandelier. Secondly, you can bet your life there's nobody locally who can play one. And third, what we want is more light in t' parish 'all."

"Er, who's the red card for, ref?"

When the village football team turned out for its first game of the season someone had forgotten to have the grass cut, or the local farmer's cows had been off their food. At any rate it was almost like an unmown meadow in the playing area.

Unfortunately the referee for that match was small and not very alert to his job, and several of his decisions were booed by the crowd. Eventually one hopeless decision stirred one of the supporters to protest volubly:

"Nay," he shouted. "Why don't they cut t' grass so t' ref can see t' game?"

An official called on a farmer about his Income Tax. He asked him how many men he had working for him. The farmer said: "Three men. I pay them £300 a week."

"Nobody else?" asked the official.

"Well," said the farmer, "there's the 'half-wit'."

"The 'half-wit'?" the official asked sharply. "How much does he get?"

"He gets £50 a week," replied the farmer, "and a new pair of corduroy trousers every six months, and, of course, he gets all his meals at the farm."

"Hm," said the official. "I'd like to see him."

"See him," said the farmer. "You're talking to him."

A Yorkshire council had just acquired a piece of waste land. Instead of having the usual reflex action and turning it into a car park, one councillor suggested having a few trees and a bit of grass on it.

Another said: "Nay, let's do the job properly and have a pool in the middle."

Someone else said: "Aye that's reet, and we'll have some mallards and fancy geese – and mebbe a gondola in with it."

"One gondola be blowed," said another. "Let's have two and let them breed."

Staying at a Whitby boarding house one summer, Pete was amused when the husband of the proprietress who acted as waiter came in one morning with some very burnt toast.

"Sorry," he said. "Something's wrong with our toaster. When the toast is done it doesn't pop up; it sends up smoke signals."

It was the end of a Yorkshire 'Wakes' holiday and two people in the homeward-bound train were 'spent up' and disconsolate. The wife sought to cheer up her husband with the glad tidings that she had "put thirty shillin' under t' candlestick before they'd coom away". But the husband refused to cheer up. "Aye, an' Ah fun' it," he snapped.

A visitor staying in a Yorkshire country house lost a valuable dog. He was very upset and inserted an advertisement in the local paper offering £250 reward for its recovery. The paper appeared, and after a few days the visitor decided to call at the newspaper office to see if there were any replies.

"I want to see the advertising manager," he said.

"He's out," said the office boy.

"Well, his assistant."

"He's out, too."

"Then I'll see the editor."

"He's out, sir."

"Great Scott," shouted the man. "Is everybody out?"

"Yes sir. They're all lookin' for this 'ere lost dog."

A proud father took his son into the local for his first pint of beer. The son, after having a sip, did not like the taste, so he said to his father:

"Dad, how long is it before beer goes flat?"

And his father replied: "I don't know, I've never left it that long."

A farmer and his daughter were loading up after market day in Skipton.

"Are them piglets in?" said he.

"All secure," said she.

"Did you collect them tools?" said he.

"Under t' seat," said she.

"We've got t' bran and t' meal?" said he.

"Ay, I think that's t' lot," said she.

"Then off we go," said he, and they jogged quietly along the road towards Grassington. Still the farmer seemed uneasy and kept on looking round into the cart.

"What's up?" said she.

"Nay, I feel uneasy somehow," said he. "As if we'd forgetten summat."

When they arrived home, he jumped down from the cart, and as he began to unload he slapped his thigh and exclaimed: "Well, I'm blessed. I know now what were bothering me. We've left yer mother i' Skipton."

A young single man was on a walking holiday in Swaledale. As he approached Muker he fell into conversation with a passing local farmer.

"I hope that Muker has some pretty girls in it."

"When you get this far up t' dale, they're all pretty."

Some years ago a small Hull coaster with a rather nervous passenger on board was steaming off the Yorkshire coast when a bad storm blew up and the vessel got into difficulties.

The captain decided to summon assistance by sending up rockets.

After the first two had been fired, a passenger went up to him and protested.

"I hope I'm not a kill-joy," he said, "but is this a time for letting off fireworks?"

A famous artist who was visiting the Dales saw an old countryman whom he thought would make a good model. So he sent his wife to bring over the man to paint him.

The old fellow hesitated.

"Will he pay me well?" he asked.

"Oh, yes; he'll probably give you a few pounds."

Still the old man hesitated. He took off his shabby hat and scratched his head in perplexity.

"It's an easy way to earn a couple of pounds," the lady prompted.

"Oh, I know that," came the reply. "I was only wondering how I'd get the paint off afterwards."

On the spur of the moment, Ned had gone away for a weekend's sea-fishing at Scarborough with his pals, but now it was Sunday and they were sat in the pub ready to go home.

"Doesn't t' Owd Book say that Jonah wor in a whale's belly for three days?" asked Ned.

"What's that to do wi' thee?" replied one of his pals.

"Nay," said Ned, "Ah were just wondering if 'is wife believed 'im when 'e got home an' told 'er where 'e'd been."

A big crowd had gathered round a man in a Yorkshire market place who was selling tins of corn cure. After a long discourse on its qualities, he asked if anyone in the crowd had bought a tin from him the week before.

From the back of the crowd came a voice: "Yes, I did."

"And did it do all I said?" asked the salesman.

"Aye, rather. My missus used it to polish t' furniture, and it took all t' knobs off t' chest o' drawers."

Overheard on the sands at Bridlington: "Eh, mother, if we'd only pawned t' other feather bed we could 'ave stayed on here over t' weekend."

A wealthy West Riding industrialist decided he had made enough money to have the first real holiday of his life. So he went on an expensive cruise, travelling first class, and providing himself with every luxury.

The first night at sea the captain sent his compliments to this distinguished passenger with an invitation to dine at the captain's table. But the industrialist was having none.

"Now, sitha lad," he said to the purser, who delivered the invitation, "Ah've paid nearly £10,000 for this trip, an' Ah'm not bahn to eat wi' t' crew, so theer."

At a function in Hull, the singing went on and on and a lot of beer was consumed. When Paul saw one of the organisers the next day, he said:

"Did you notice me spending £100 last night?"

His pal replied: "You certainly seemed to be enjoying yourself."

He thought for a while and said: "That's a relief – I thought I'd lost it."

A visitor to a Selby pub was flabbergasted to see a native ordering pint by pint at intervals of a few minutes and 'swallacking' each pint as soon as it was served.

"Do you always drink your beer like that?" asked the astonished visitor.

"Only since mi accident," came the reply.

"Your accident?"

"Aye, mi accident. I once had a pint knocked ovver."

Part of a conversation overheard while passing a local inn, from which came the loud and mournful wailing of a 'singer' of doubtful talent. Two men came out of the pub:

"Cum on, let's goer darn ter t' Red Lion. We mun as weel be beaten up as de-efened."

An argument had arisen during a game of snooker in the local pub as to whether two balls were touching.

"Tha can see from 'ere, white un's touchin' but t' red un in't," said an old boy in the corner.

Vicar to village reprobate: "I am pleased, John, that you have turned over a new leaf. I saw you at our temperance meeting last night."

John: "So that's where I were last neet, I mun tell t' wife."

A fellwalker entered a Dales inn and got into conversation with a local farmer.

"Will you have another one?" asked the walker, after several glasses of ale had been drunk.

"Nay," was the reply. "Ah munnat stop. Ah've t' van outside wi' t' lambs, sheep and t' missus in it."

In the West Riding a man called at a country inn and asked for a glass of beer.

"Looks like rain," said the sociable landlord.

"Aye," was the reply, "an' it tastes like it, too."

A group of anglers were relating their experiences in the bar of a Wharfedale inn.

"I was once fishing on a Scottish loch and caught one so big that the others wouldn't let me haul it into the boat in case it swamped us."

"Oh aye," said an old dalesman. "Same thing 'appened to me once when I were on t' *Queen Elizabeth*."

Overheard on a Bradford bus late one night, as two drinking friends parted: "Ah'll see thee Sunda' mornin' then, Fred."

"Sunda' mornin'," exclaimed Fred. "Ah nivver knew they 'ad em."

When a rather bow-legged stranger called in at the local one evening, he promptly took up a place in front of the fire in the traditional manner warming his rear. No-one objected, as obviously he had been walking some distance in the rain and was very wet.

After he had occupied the place for the best part of an hour, however, Owd Kit (whose proper place it was) thought it about time he moved. So he went across to the stranger, tapped him on the shoulder and pointed to his legs.

"Sitha, lad," he said. "Move thissen back a bit. Tha's warping."

In an attempt to cut down the accident rate, Yorkshire Television put out a notice persuading the Dales folk to wear something white so they could be seen on the roads.

One farmer took this very seriously. He bought white boots, white trousers, and a white mac, a white flat cap and even a white stick. One dark winter's night he set out to walk to Gunnerside – and was knocked down by a snowplough.

The queue in the post office was getting longer and longer. At its head, before the grille labelled 'Pensioners', an old lady was taking her time. She fumbled in her handbag, brought first one and then another article out, and laid them on the counter. They made an imposing collection.

The pension book still hadn't come to light, but an old man with a soldierly look could bear it no longer. He called out "Hurry up, Ma. This is a pay parade, not a kit inspection."

An old carrier's cart was ambling along an East Riding road one dark night. A large car approached and the driver dipped his headlights to avoid dazzling the carrier.

"George," exclaimed that worthy to his companion. "We mun return t' compliment. Just blow out that offside candle."

A farmer surprised his neighbours by selling an old, battered van and buying a new Rolls-Royce.

"And how are you liking your new car?" a friend inquired.

"Fine," replied the farmer.

"What is it about the Rolls that suits you best, then?"

The farmer considered before replying.

"Why, now, I'd say it's the glass screen between front and rear… it's nice being able to drive without the cows licking t' back o' mi neck."

Many years ago a farmer, driving his horse and trap from Pickering market, was stopped by a young policeman.

"Now what's wrang?" asked the farmer.

"Do you know you are driving without lights?"

"Aye," said the farmer. "But does thou know that Ah's as tight as a bottle, and tawd mare's as blind as a bat, sae what's good o' lights tae us?"

Three of the village elders were gazing at the fells around the green when one said: "Isn't yon one of Seth Brown's cows?"

A long pause followed while they all gazed at the animal.

"Nay," said the second. "Tha's talking daft. That's one of Kit Cornthwaite's."

Upon which the third man rose as hastily as his eighty years would allow, and remarked with indignation: "Nay, if thee two are going to argify, I'm bahn home." And home he went.

The decline of Sheffield Wednesday had been apparent to many, but it was brought home very forcibly at a sparsely attended match.

An irate father, turning to his small son who had lost all interest in the game and was performing alarming gymnastics on a deserted crush barrier, shouted: "Behave thisen, or I'll mak thee cum 'ere again."

*"Hello, Childline?...Listen, me dad's threatened to
take me to Sheffield Wednesday again..."*

An elderly lady carefully climbed onto the bus and asked the driver to go steadily as she was going to the infirmary. When she alighted, the conductor helped her off the bus and asked if all was well.

The old lady replied: "I just made a jelly to take to the infirmary, and it hadn't quite set when I left home."

Soon after the arrival of his first baby, the Dales farmer's wife went upstairs one evening and found him standing by the cot gazing earnestly at it. She was very touched by the sight, and tears filled her eyes. Her arm stole softly round him. He started slightly at the touch, and she asked him what he was thinking. "Nay, lass," he said, sadly. "It beats me how they can reckon to ask £100 for a cot like that."

A village lad on one of his rare visits to the town, went to buy a cap.

"What size?" asked the assistant.

"Ee, Ah doan't knaw," said the lad. "But me brother taks a six an' seven eighths, an' Ah'm older na him, soa as'll tak eight an' nine tenths – an' gie me one o' them theer wi' a neb at t' side."

'Old Sara' was a forthright Daleswoman and had a horror of doctors. Being in failing health, she was persuaded to visit the local doctor. On her return she described her experience.

"He gat ma set doon on a reight comfortable chair, an' he told ma to tak' me bloose off. When Ah wor hawf neaked, he popped yan end of a telephone thing on to mi chest and he listened in at t' other end. Then he tapped me all ovver an' teld ma to put mi cloas back on.

"Ya nivver heeard such questions he asked ma. I answered as weeal as Ah could. Then 'e says sudden like: ' 'Ow hev yer been sleeping lately, Sara?' 'Why,' Ah ses, 'wi' mi back to Charlie, seeam as Ah've done for years.' "

Paul was walking one morning along a Pennine summit when he saw an old man mending a drystone wall. It was a glorious day; the hills shone green near at hand, blue in the distance. Paul nodded to the old chap and said "Fine morning."

The old man gave him a glance of scorn and said witheringly: "Well, don't let's get into a lather about it."

When TV first came to Yorkshire, an elderly lady from upper Wharfedale was visited by a TV salesman. She was moderately interested, but when he asked if she would like to install a set in her cottage, her reply was: "Nay, Ah don't want all sorts of folk like you have on there coming into my room, acting foolishly and talking rubbish. Besides, Ah don't want folk Ah've never met before looking out o' that box at all my bits and pieces."

A rather shy girl entered the library van and paused as if lost.

"What book would you like?" asked the librarian in charge.

"Where do you keep 'Romance'?" asked the girl.

Said the male librarian helpfully: "You'll find Romance in that little dark corner, miss."

And a very embarrassed male borrower already in the dark corner moved away quickly.

Two old-aged pensioners passed their time sitting on the seats in Bradford's Forster Square every day watching the world go by. One of them left his friend to go home after their daily session and wasn't seen by his pal at the usual place for about six months.

Eventually he turned up and his friend asked him where he had been.

"Nay, Ah wor pulled in on a identification parade at t' police station an' a blonde said: 'That's him.' Ah wor so prahd o' misen, Ah pleaded guilty, an' gate six months."

"I'm t' new farmhand – any grub?"

A North Yorkshire farmer was boasting about a new set of dentures he had just obtained from his dentist.

"They're real good 'uns," he told his neighbour. "Ah've to tek 'em out for eatin', like, but for market day and going about, like, they're champion."

A North Yorkshire roadman won quite a substantial prize in the National Lottery. Yet his friends were surprised that, instead of being pleased, he was very gloomy about it.

"Why, Kit, what's the matter?" asked a pal.

"Nay," he said. "Ah've wasted gooid money on t' other ticket. Why Ah ever bought two beats me."

Grandad was sitting muttering to himself as he peeled some very dirty potatoes. Suddenly he paused, looked up and said to his daughter: "Ee, lass. Thi sent that much work on these 'ere 'taties 'till thi'll 'ave noa farms left in a bit."

A farmer a few miles from York met another farmer in the city who said to him: "Why, yer going to lose that man o' yours aren't you?"

"Not 'at Ah know of. He's said nowt to me aboot it yet."

"Oh yes," answered the other. "He's coming to oor pleeace in a few weeks time – what sort of a man is he?"

"Oh well, he's a rare hand wi' a fork," was the answer.

"That'll just suit me, fer haytime an' harvest."

"But Ah meean at t' table."

When Leeds War Memorial was unveiled a great crowd gathered. An elderly lady collapsed and with a good deal of difficulty was carried through the crowd by two St John Ambulance men. Then the patient suddenly recovered.

"I'm all reet now," she told her bearers. "But tha knaws I'm over seventy, an' it wor the only way I could get to t' front."

A certain market town in Yorkshire has a clock tower in the square. Close by is a public letter box. A jovial citizen of the place staggered up to the mail box, dropped a penny into the slot and then glanced at the illuminated clock face.

"Heck," he said. "Ah'm nine pounds overweight."

A minister's wife while calling on a member of the congregation who was married to a farmer, mentioned with excusable pride that her daughter had won the first prize in a local beauty competition.

Immediately the farmer's wife showed her fellow feeling.

"I can understand your pride," she said. "Eeh, I can remember how pleased I was when t' owd pig took t' first prize at t' agricultural show.

Some old ladies in Sowerby recounted watching highlights of a television programme. It was the wedding of Princess Alexandra, and one old lady had pointed to Prince Philip and said: "Who's yon chap?" To which another old lady replied: "That's 'im 'at t' Queen lives wi'."

Her parents decided that it was time little Ann started attending church. The following Sunday, she accompanied them to the service. The minister, high in his pulpit, was earnest and vigorous. His voice rolled out over his flock as he waved his arms and twisted his body here and there. The small girl was completely fascinated. At last, clutching her father's arm, she asked anxiously: "What do we do if he gets out?"

During a drought early in the summer, prayers for rain were spoken by the preacher at a Methodist chapel in Wensleydale.

Afterwards a member of the congregation said: "Steady on a bit with your prayers for rain; we need another two dry days to get t' hay in."

In the 1930s there was an amateur concert party which used to perform mainly at church socials. One winter Saturday evening they arrived at a little church where they were to perform in the church hall, and were met by the verger.

"Theer's t' dressin' room," he said, indicating a small vestry.

"Dressing room?" one queried, "but there are ladies and gentlemen in the party."

"Well," replied the old man belligerently, "what's matter? 'A they 'ad words or summat?"

A farmer's wife went into a picture dealer's and asked to see a still life. Eventually she chose one representing a bouquet of flowers, a plate of ham and a roll.

"How much?" she enquired.

"It's very cheap, £25."

"But I saw one just like it the other day for £15."

"It couldn't have been as good as this, madam."

"Indeed, it was even better. There was a lot more ham on the plate."

The weather was very cold one winter, and the organist of a small Yorkshire church reprimanded the caretaker (who was also the organ-blower) for not having the church sufficiently heated. "It's almost too cold for me to play the organ," he grumbled.

After the service, the organ-blower was heard laughing and said: "He's allus hevving a go at me, but I got me revenge toneet. When he were playing 'Christians Awake' I were blowing for 'God rest ye Merry Gentlemen'."

Retired Dales labourer replying to another who had just said he could see a fly on the church clockface: "Ah wish he'd stop clumpin' about up there. Ah can't hear misen think."

A Methodist chapel was badly in need of repair, so the minister called a meeting and explained that at least £500 would be needed to put things right.

Immediately a wealthy but stingy member of the congregation rose to his feet, and said that he would be glad to contribute £5 to the effort.

Just as he sat down a lump of plaster fell from the ceiling and hit him on the top of his head, whereupon the need for repairs being more forcibly impressed upon him than by the minister's appeal, he hastily rose again and said that he had made a mistake. What he would contribute to the renovation fund was £50.

This was too much for an enthusiastic brother who immediately called out: "Hallelujah. Hit him again, Lord, hit him again."

In the old days, there was such rivalry between North-country chapels of various denominations that, at the end of the evening performance in each place, an expectant hush descended.

A steward mounted the steps to the pulpit, holding a piece of paper and announcing how much had been raised by the collections in that particular chapel.

"Aye," he boasted, "and that's £20 more than t' Wesleyans – and £22 more than Bethel."

You couldn't do better than that.

THE BATTLE OF THE SEXES

marital discord – domestic bliss –
keeping up appearances – womanly wiles

The romantic interaction of men and women is ripe for
humour, especially in Yorkshire: somehow, from Bridlington in the east to Hebden Bridge in the west, we're not really
very good at it. We're strong silent types or we're garrulous to
the point of linguistic incontinence but we always seem to get
the tone ever so slightly wrong.

I've been married to the same lovely woman for three
decades but I know that, because we're from Yorkshire, we
have to tread carefully in matters of the heart. In the year we
got married I sent her a Valentine card that I thought was so
funny I could hardly pay for it for laughing. On the front was
a picture of an old lady in a headscarf with her false teeth
missing, and the words "You're the kind of girl I could take
home to mother…" and inside the card a hilarious gag "…she
could do with a good laugh!" My wife sat me down and told
me, in no uncertain terms, never to send her a Valentine again,
and I haven't. I still think it's a great gag.

One of our first dates was at the old Co-op Café in
Barnsley. You had to stand at the front and wait to be seated,
common enough practice these days but seen as a ridiculous
Southern custom in Barnsley in the mid-seventies. Why
couldn't tha just sit down and shout across t' room? I knew
from my extensive reading of James Bond novels that I had to
say "Table for two, please," and let my wife go first. The waitress approached. I forgot what to say. My mind was like a bowl

of custard before the first spoon plunges in: virgin territory with nothing disturbing it. Nothing as important as a thought, anyway.

The waitress, a woman who looked old enough to be my mam (but looked a bit like my dad), kept staring at me, her smile a rictus on her painted face. I opened my mouth. "Table for both," I said. I knew that didn't sound right. "Table for us," I said, and the tone was wrong, clanking like a chipped bell. I tried again "Table for these. Table for this. Table for her and him." Eventually my wife helped me out, as she's done many times ever since. "Table for two," she said. We had a lovely meal but then it was time to choose the pudding. I knew from my reading that sophisticates had cheese and biscuits after their dinner although for the life of me I couldn't think why, especially since I was already full. Still, I thought I'd have a go. "I'll have the cheese, please," I said. The waitress said, in a voice that hovered between the posh and the Rotherham: "I'll just go and check what we have available, sir." Nobody had ever called me sir before, except when I had a walk-on part as Walter Raleigh in a school play. She came back smiling triumphantly. "We've got the red or the white, sir," she said.

That tale sounds like it comes from the mists of time but last year my wife and I were in a café in Sheffield; the lad behind the bar looked like the grandson of the waitress from the old Co-op Café. "We'll have the soup," I said, my voice masterful and commanding, and then I followed up with "What is the soup?" He said: "I'll just check for you," and he nipped into the kitchen and came back with a smile: "It's soup of the day," he said. I'll have the cheese.

This chapter is a manual of how not to act on a date, of how not to impress a member of the opposite sex. The following pages overflow with music-hall characters, with people from comic postcards and, let's face it, people from jokes. At the back of all these gags is deep, abiding, unending love. And that's Yorkshire love, which is the strongest of all. Hey: that would make a good slogan for a teatowel! I'll have a word with my friends at *Dalesman*.

Ian McMillan

The husband drew his chair up beside his wife's sewing machine and began a series of running comments: "Don't you think it's running too fast? Look out, or you'll have the needle through your finger."

"Why, what on earth's the matter with you?" demanded his wife presently. "I've been running this machine for years."

"Oh," said the husband. "I was only trying to help you sew as you often help me to drive the car."

A Dales schoolteacher had punished Tommy so often for talking during school, and the punishments had been so apparently without effect, that as a last resort she decided to notify Tommy's father of his son's fault. So, following the deportment mark on his next report, there were these words: 'Tommy talks a great deal'.

In due time the report was returned with his father's signature. Under it was written: 'You ought to hear his mother'.

Hearing that a man in a Yorkshire village had reached the age of a hundred, the reporter interviewed his wife on the subject.

"You must be very proud of him," he remarked. "Oh, I don't know," was the reply. "The only thing he's ever done is grow old, and he's taken a mighty long time over that."

A veteran farmer in the East Riding remarked: "I only once had a holiday, as you might say. That was when t' wife went off with the lodger. But it didn't last so long; you see she soon came back."

"*Nice mane on her – good firm rump, too.*"
"*Aye, but what aboot t' horse?*"

An old couple who kept the village shop were disturbed from their sleep in the early hours by the sound of someone moving about below.

The wife said to her husband: "I think you'd best go down and see what's happening."

Her husband quickly replied: "Nay lass, thee go, they'll noan touch thee. Thou's littler than me."

Smallholder describing how weak his wife was after an illness: "The fact is, doctor, she really isn't fit to serve t' pigs."

Sally and her friend went to Belle Vue Zoo on their day off. After enjoying the gardens and birds, they went to watch the monkeys. One large male was bounding about, rattling the bars, and eventually beating his head in rage on the floor of the cage.

At that moment Sally turned to her friend and said: "Oh, dear. That reminds me. I shall have to tell my husband tonight that I've scratched a wing of the car."

One old farmer asked another if he was going to the gala and fancy dress parade. The second old man said: "No."

"But," said the first, "I've heard there's a lass going as Lady Godiva with nowt on, riding on a white hoss."

The second old man pricked up his ears at this and said: "I think I'll come. It's a long time since I've seen a white hoss."

Into the village police station ran a very pretty lady, in tears.

Throwing a photograph down on the desk, she appealed to the sergeant in charge.

"My husband has disappeared," she sobbed. "There is his picture. I want you to find him."

The sergeant studied the photograph for a while. Then he looked up. "Why?" he asked.

Susan, who had been married only a few weeks, asked her husband to sample her first attempt at making plum jam.

"Well, what do you think of it?" she asked.

"It lacks summat," he replied. "Flavour, I think."

A miner who had overslept was hurriedly getting dressed for his day shift.

"Alf," said his wife in a voice like a whiplash. "Tha's putting thi clogs on t' wrong feet."

"Ah know," said he. "They ought to be on thine."

Joe the gardener worked well but was always very downcast on Friday afternoons. The explanation came when he asked if he could be paid monthly instead of weekly.

When asked why, he replied: "Well, you see, the missus and me always has an awful row every payday."

A man wanted a divorce from his wife because she kept goats. The solicitor said this gave him no grounds for divorce.

"Oh, but she keeps them in t' bedroom and they smell."

Her solicitor said: "Couldn't you open the window?"

"What," said the applicant, "and let all my pigeons out?"

A man dashed into a Dales police station at midnight.

"Mi wife," he gasped. "Will you find mi wife. She's been missing since eight this evening. I must find her."

"Particulars?" asked the sergeant: "Height?"

"I – I don't know."

"Do you know how she was dressed?"

"No, but she took t' dog with her."

"What kind of dog?"

"Brindle bull terrier, weight 53 lbs, four dark blotches on his body shading from grey to white, three white legs, and right front leg brindled. A small nick in his left ear."

When Joe was celebrating his eightieth birthday with a party, a newspaper reporter asked him what was his recipe for so long a life.

"Contentment," said Joe.

"So you have had a contented and happy life," said the reporter. "No domestic troubles?"

"No," said Joe. "When t' wife starts to natter, I goes inter t' garden. If Ah'm wrong side out, she goes inter t' kitchen."

"Well," said the reporter, "you look well."

"Yes," said Joe. "I spend a lot of time in t' garden."

An old Dalesman was very much hen-pecked. Unfortunately, his wife had inherited a lot of the furniture and silver in the house, and she was always reminding him that they were hers.

One night she was awakened by a strange noise downstairs. She roused her husband: "James," she said, "get up quickly and go downstairs, there are burglars in the house."

"Burglars," said Smith, turning over to go to sleep again, "well let 'em burgle; there's nothing of mine down there."

Train conversation overheard near York between two ladies:

"I can't see whatever fun you find, dear, in going on those fishing expeditions with your husband. I know I should find it awfully tiresome."

"Oh, that's simply because you don't understand anything about fishing."

"But do you understand anything about it yourself?"

"Understand? Why, of course I do, and it's perfectly lovely. I just sit in the stern of the boat, and give George advice; and when he loses a fish, I carefully explain to him what he ought to have done to prevent its getting away."

"But I shouldn't think, dear, there's any fun in that?"

"No, perhaps you wouldn't, dear, if you didn't know how mad it makes George every time."

A middle-aged bachelor, living on his own in a Yorkshire village, was a shrewd character with a keen sense of humour but naturally very set in his ways.

He was asked if he had ever considered getting married and enjoying the comforts of the connubial state.

He pondered for a short while and then replied:

"Well, I have thought about it from time to time, but have always decided against it on the grounds that any women who would be daft enough to marry me would be too daft for me to marry."

A man in a West Riding town was met by a workmate as he was on his way to the mill.

"Tha saands ter 'ev a lot o' brass," said the friend as they walked along.

"Brass be blowed," was the reply, "it's mi wife's false teeth. There's too much being 'etten at ahr 'ouse between meals."

A small boy, living at Sutton-in-Craven, was sent by his mother, early one morning, to a neighbouring farm, to borrow something.

Seeing the farmer milking in the cowshed, he enquired: "Is t' missus in?"

"She's in bed," the farmer replied, "and thee don't go disturbin' 'er. The first thing she'll do will be to leet a candle, then she'll come dahnstairs and leet a fire. Next she'll put t' kettle on and make hersen some teea, then she'll want summat to eeat. Let 'er alone, she's costing nowt theer."

It was spring-cleaning time, and a group of pals had escaped to the local pub. "Ah don't know which is t' worst to live wi'," commented one. "A woman that's too lazy to fettle up when it's needed, or one that's allus fettlin' whether t' house needs it or not."

He stood at the fountain-pen counter of a Bradford store making a careful choice.

"You see," he explained to the assistant, "I'm buying a present for my wife."

"A surprise, perhaps?" replied the assistant.

"I'll say so," was the answer. "She's expecting a new car."

An old Whitby couple had lived a cat-and-dog life and had not spoken to each other for years. In the course of time the husband fell ill and lay dying. His wife, anxious for a reconciliation before it was too late, decided to make the first advance. She went upstairs to the old man's bedside and, breaking the long, long silence, said:

"Aaron, where does thee want to be buried?"

The answer came back without hesitation and in a voice full of malice: "Atop o' thee."

Woman talking to another about men: "Afore yer married he'll lift ye over a puddle, but after he'll look round to see if you've fallen in t' beck."

The landlady at the Dales village inn served Jack with his pint of ale. She winked at the others and said to the old man: "It's time you got a wife. Haven't you ever thought about it?"

Back came the immediate reply: "Ah'd a fancy for thee once, missus. Aye, thou was a bonnie lass then."

One day a clergyman visited a house and found a man and his wife having what is known in some parts as a 'reight fratch'.

"Come, come," said the minister, "this won't do."

He then pointed to the hearth where the cat was sleeping by the dog: "Just look at these two, how peaceful they are."

"Aye," said the Dalesman, "but thee tee 'em together and then see what happens."

In a Dales village a conjurer was appearing at the village hall. Amos bought his wife a ticket for the show.

"Maggie," said Amos, "here's a ticket for tonight's conjuring show. When the conjurer comes to that part where he takes a teaspoonful of flour and one egg and makes twenty omelettes, watch verra verra close."

A Sedbergh tradesman joined a local farmer who by his dirt bespattered condition had evidently visited the auction mart.

"By, Jack," said tradesman Ted. "Thoo's a ter'ble mess; whatever'll t' missis say when she siz tha?"

"Neea, I don't knaa," replied Jack, looking somewhat melancholy at the thought.

"I'll tell tha what," said Ted, pointing at the nearby greengrocer's window with its bright display of blooms. "Tak her some flowers."

"Floowers!" exclaimed Jack in amazement. "But she's not deead."

Two lads, Jack and Bill, were brought up in the same village and were very close pals all their school days. Afterwards they had to go out to earn their living, and they drifted wide apart. It was many years before they saw each other again.

At last they met, and Jack says to Bill: "Hello Bill, how's ta going on. Ah hear thou's married. What's t' wife like?"

"Oh," says Bill, "she's a little angel. What's thine like?"

"Nay," says Jack. "Mine isn't deead yet."

The old Dalesman was late home, as usual. His wife asked: "What's ta bin dewin?"

"Ah've bin at a beer-drinkin' competishun," he replied.

She knew who would be the winner, but she asked: "An' who got t' second?"

He immediately answered "Your sister."

A farmer describing a neighbour's wife to a friend: "Oh she's a good un alright, got a face on 'er like a kind old hoss."

A Dales doctor spoke to a patient: "Do you know you've been going about with a bone broken?" he asked. "Why didn't you come to me before?"

"Well," was the reply. "Every time Ah says something is wrang wi' me, t' wife maks me stop smoking."

In a West Yorkshire court, a woman was giving evidence in a motoring case: "I was driving down the street with my husband at the wheel."

In a Hawes café, a farmer's wife was telling her friend that her husband had just stopped smoking.

"My goodness, that takes some will-power I think," said her friend.

"Indeed it does dear," agreed the wife. "And that's just what I've got."

Joe and his wife, after an even hotter row than usual, sat sulking, he on one side of the fire, she on the other, with the cat on the rug between them.

When it seemed that the sullen silence would never be broken, Joe slowly uncrossed, then recrossed his legs, sighed and said "Ee, Ah wish one of us three were deead. An' Ah doan't meean misen."

Just then the cat looked and mewed. "Ah doon't meean thee, nawther," said Joe.

Sammy was chatting with friends one evening when one of his companions remarked that some of his friends were henpecked. He promptly replied: "Eeh, but it's grand bein' pecked by t' reight 'en."

An old dame was heard giving advice to a young 'ovver-fond' bride: "Never put thi husband on a pedestal. He'll nobbut want dusting."

On the way home through Skipton, a couple gave a lift to an airman returning to camp and mentioned that they had just been to the Dales. He remarked that by coincidence he would be going there the following week.

As he was in the forces, they asked if he was going on some sort of training course,

"Well, you could put it that way," he replied. "It's my honeymoon."

An East Riding man, troubled by his wife's reckless way with money, finally gave her an account book and £100 for the housekeeping.

"Now," he said. "Thoo put down what Ah've gi'en thoo on one page, and on t' opposite page put down what thoo's done wi' it. Then thoo'll know wheer all t' money's gone."

At the end of the week she presented the book eagerly to her husband. "Look, I've done just as you told me."

And she had. On one page was written: '£100 received'. On the opposite page was written: 'Spent it all'.

Dave attended a lavish function with his wife. And the welcome presence of the free bar was like manna from Heaven. His gait became unsteadier as the evening progressed, and eventually his long-suffering spouse decided to shame him into some semblance of sobriety. She made sure everyone in the room heard her objection as she hollered:

"Dave, that must be the tenth time you have been to the bar for a large whisky. Doesn't it embarrass you?"

"Why should I be embarrassed, my love? I keep telling the barman the drinks are for you."

Three farmer brothers lived together in happy bachelordom, being well cared for by their elder sister, who acted as house-keeper, and made a good job of it. Then came the unhappy day when she passed away.

On the evening of the funeral the trio sat round the fireside and discussed the situation, at last arriving at the unanimous conclusion that one of them must get married. Which should it be? was the question.

"Well, I'm too old," said the elder brother. "And I'm too delicate," said the second.

"It's just as I expected," said the third. "It's always the same if there's anything unpleasant to be done – it's always me that has it to do."

Heard at a W I meeting:

"And how is your husband getting on?"

"I hardly know. He's so busy I only see him for about an hour a day."

"Oh, you poor thing, I am sorry."

"Oh, that's all right. The hour soon passes."

Ted listened patiently as his wife grumbled away at all his shortcomings. She ended up with "...and I've a good mind to leave you."

"Well, let me know when you're going," he replied, "and I'll take you."

"Did you hear that owd Dick Horsfall's gettin' wed again?" said Sam in the local.

"You'd have thought he were owd enough to know better nor that."

"Aye, he does know better, lad," said Bill. "But trouble is he met a widder who knew better still."

A Yorkshire bishop detected one of his servants in a lie. "You know, my man," he said. "One far greater than either of us notices everything we do."

"Yes, my lord bishop," replied the man. "My wife has already spoken to me about it."

When a Wharfedale wife asked her husband what he would like her to buy him for his birthday, he replied:

"That's all right, love, but Ah don't think Ah can afford it this year."

Harassed woman to very deaf husband: "Oh I do wish you would wear your hearing-aid."

"But I do lass," he replied. "I wear it many a time when I'm by myself."

A married couple were at a friend's wedding.

"The women always look beautiful at weddings," she said, "but the men always look scared."

He replied: "They'll both get ovver it."

Brian was singing the praises of his new girlfriend to his friend: "She's as different from other women as a fine brandy is to beer."

"Aye, but you get t' same kind of headache from both on 'em."

OFF-CUMED UNS

visitors – Southerners –
newcomers – Lancastrians

There's a (possibly) apocryphal story about two brothers from Barnsley who went to London on the train for a day out. Wandering down Oxford Street, one of the lads got separated from the other. He looked around for a while then walked up to a complete stranger somewhere near Oxford Circus tube station and said: "Eyop: has tha seen our big 'un?" It may not be true but I like to think it is.

We like visitors and incomers in Yorkshire and we've always welcomed people from all over the world to the sacred shire, but, let's face it, we're always a bit suspicious of the South and Southerners, and we really don't get people from Lancashire. I mean, they live in the next county to Yorkshire: why don't they all just move over here? What's the point in living there when you could live here?

I like Lancashire, actually, but I find you can't get a cup of tea out of them. You go back to their house and they say: "Do you not want a cup of tea?" and you say: "I don't know: you've not asked me yet." And they say: "Have you not had one?" "Will you not be having one?" "You'll not have had one?" Very strange. Just get the flaming kettle on! Mind you, they're not as odd as people from North Derbyshire who call their house their arse. "I've just had double glazing fitted in my arse, youth!" Have you really?

The South, though. That's a foreign land and, as far as Yorkshire humour is concerned, a deep, deep well. Yorkshire and the South don't understand each other, and that's the way we like it. I once went with my son to watch the mighty Barnsley FC play Gillingham. The bus dropped us some way from the ground and me and my lad wandered through the terraced streets. A door opened and a skinny man in a white shirt popped out. " 'Ere! You from Barnsley?" he said, his voice as thin as his chest: he sounded like chalk screeching on a black-board. I nodded. My son looked worried. "It's okay, I won't hurt yer!" he squeaked. He shouted indoors: " 'ere, Cuppa Tea! Two people from Barnsley here!" His mate, the oddly named Cuppa Tea, stuck his head round the door. He was as fat as the first guy was thin; he looked like Humpty Dumpty in a Gillingham shirt. Cuppa Tea gazed at us curiously. "They look just like us, don't they?" he said. They examined us like they were examining fossils of cro-magnon man. "Ask 'em, Cuppa, ask 'em!" said the thin man. The fat bloke looked me in the eye and said: " 'Ere: is it true that when your tea's too hot you waft it with your cap and when it's too cold you wrap your muffler round the cup?" I nodded and said: "Of course it is," and the two men laughed, cheered and high-fived.

So let's put our cards on the table. This globe is divided in two: people who are from Yorkshire on the one hand, and sad people on the other hand. What we're talking about here isn't just people from Yorkshire versus people from Lancashire, or people from Yorkshire versus people from the South. It's Yorkshire against the World. Mind you, let's not start on people from North Yorkshire against people from South Yorkshire, or West Yorkshire types compared to Malton denizens. And, as I'm from Darfield near Barnsley, please don't ask me about people from Wombwell. Especially the top end of Wombwell. Especially the right-hand side of the top end of Wombwell. Especially the upper section of the right-hand side of the top end of Wombwell. Just don't ask me.

Ian McMillan

In a distant outpost of Empire, where English were out numbered by Scots and Welsh, an enthusiast decided to try to start a Society of Yorkshiremen.

When he came to his pal for support, he suggested that the numbers would hardly suffice. "Why not," he said, "have a Yorkshire and Lancashire Society, such as they have in some places."

"Some places," was the reply, "they have cat and dog shows."

A Canadian who was over here during the last war has returned to stay with some Yorkshire friends.

He visited a place in the East Riding where he had been all those years ago. He stopped a native and said: "The last time I was here you had two windmills in this place. Now there's only one. What happened to the other one?"

"Oh," said the Yorkshireman, "tha sees, there wasn't enuff wind for t' two on 'em, so we pulled one down."

A soldier from North of the Border made the acquaintance of a girl in a Yorkshire town where he was stationed. He courted her for some time and eventually plucked up enough courage to propose to her but found it a little difficult.

"I was here on Monday night, wasn't I, Mary?" he began.

"Of course."

"And I was here again on Tuesday night?"

"That's so."

"And I was back again on Wednesday night?"

"You were, Ian."

"Now this is Friday and here I am again. Oh, Mary, d'ye no smell a rat?"

Recently Tess, a Yorkshire lass, had an Irish friend to stay with her. Tess asked what impressed her most, and she replied: "The people. Everyone calls me 'Luv'."

A young Finnish doctor came to Scotland to add to his medical knowledge. At first he could not speak English, but he soon acquired a working knowledge of it. Later on he was sent to Bradford and on hearing the Yorkshire dialect thought he had arrived in another country. However, he persevered with what to him was a new language and it was not long before he was saying to his patient: "Nah, lad, open thi gob and let's have a lewk at thi lollicker."

Many Italian and Polish women were once employed in various textile mills in the West Riding. One employer of these took his customary walk into the weaving shed during the morning. Meeting the shed overlooker, he remarked: "I didn't know we had any Chinese woman here."

To which the overlooker said: "We haven't. What makes you think that?"

The boss replied: "I heard one woman call out 'Whowashy-wee,' and another said 'Shewer-wee-ersen.' "

It took a bit of explaining that they were discussing another of their workmates whom they had seen on her way to the cinema the previous night.

One day a large American limousine drew up in the centre of a Yorkshire village alongside one of the older residents. An American voice hailed the old rustic: "Say guy, I guess I'm a little lost. Can you tell me the way to Leeds."

The old resident stood a few seconds and then answered slowly: "Noah, Ah can't."

The American then said: "Well, now, maybe you can tell me the way to York?"

"Noah," replied the old boy.

The man in the car appeared a little upset and said rather sharply: "You sure don't know much, do you?"

"Noah," replied the countryman. "Bud Ah's noorn lost."

A town-dwelling couple had moved recently to a more rural area. The wife had felt obliged to reprimand the new milkman whose deliveries were apt to be haphazard.

One morning she opened the door and found a milkless doorstep plus a cow grazing placidly in the back garden. Despondently she remarked to her husband: "Ah'm afeared yon milkman's taken t' huff. He's left us a do-it-yoursen kit."

Albert came home from the mill looking cross and when asked what had gone wrong, he said: "Nay, Ah reckon nowt to working wi' foreigners in t' mill."

"Well," said his wife, "we have to be tolerant nowadays. You'll have to put up with them if it's giving them a better life than they had in their own country."

"Aye, that's all reet," said Albert," but fancy starting fellers fra' Scunthorpe – what the 'ell do they know about weaving theer?"

The new Dales vicar met one of his parishioners in the village.

"Do you know where you could find me a nice treble, Thomas?" he asked.

Thomas looked nervously round.

"Well, sir," he replied. "What be you thinking about – the choir or racing?"

Stewart was on an angling holiday in Wharfedale and decided on his first morning to start early. By five o'clock he was striding down to the river with rod and sandwiches, very proud of his ability to 'get agate' before the rest of the world was up.

Turning a bend in the road he almost bumped into a farm man coming the other way.

"Good morning," Stewart said brightly. "It's very nice to be out and about."

"Aye, it is," he replied. "But it were cold first thing."

A teacher from north of the border was taking a class of Yorkshire schoolboys for a lesson and he offered a prize of £5 for the best answer to the question: "Who is the greatest man in history?"

Tommy replied: "Robert the Bruce, sir."

Patting him on the head, the teacher handed over the money without demur.

"But what was your reason for the answer you gave?" he asked.

Tommy: "Well, Ah knoa deep dahn i' me awn 'eart 'at Ah should 'ave said Freddie Trueman, but business is business."

Ronnie had commented on the curious ways of the folk who lived in a village not far from his home when a local stopped him with the exclamation: "Ay, but there's villages, and villages and some is better than others. Ah always says that the higher you go up t' hill, the queerer folk is. Mark my words, you'll always find that true."

When the son of a Yorkshire farmer had to visit London to attend an interview, his Dad gave him careful instructions about using the Underground trains.

On the boy's return, the father enquired:

"How didst fare in t' Tube, lad?"

"Ah got a taxi, Dad," said the son.

"My, that'd cost a bit," explained the older man.

"Nay, 't were cheap. Then man asked fer two and ninepence so I gived him three bob. He looked hard at me and said: 'I bet you come from Yorkshire,' so I said, 'Aye, an' Ah'm waiting fer mi threepence.' "

Overheard at the York Mystery Plays: two Americans were watching a Yorkshire dialect play, and one remarked: "Oh, George, they talk just like they do in *Dalesman*."

A city girl was on her first visit to the North York Moors. She was anxious to show that she was not altogether ignorant of rural conditions, and when a dish of honey was set before her on the breakfast table she saw her opportunity.

"Oh," she observed casually. "I see you keep a bee."

One summer afternoon the old men of a Dales village were on the green chatting over the death of an old friend when along came a newcomer to express his sorrow at the death of the old villager, who had lived there since his early youth.

"It is sad when an old native of the village dies," said the new resident. "Nay lad, he wasn't a native, 'e was a come-er-in-a," said one of the old men who had lived in the village all his life. " 'E only lived here seventy year."

Many years ago a Sheffield man used to go on weekend fishing trips up in Dentdale, where he had a small stone cottage. He became a welcome visitor at the local village pub.

One evening, walking home with a farmer and coming to his cottage, the man asked the farmer to come in and share a bottle of beer. "Nay, nay, Mester. A man 'as can't sup enough before t' pub shuts, is either poorly, or he doesn't know when he's 'ad enough."

Two Yorkshiremen had taken rather too much to drink. As they stumbled along a country road, they had a heated argument about what they saw in the heavens.

One asserted it was the sun. The other was equally certain it was the moon.

Seeing another man approaching, they appealed to him.

One of them said: "Ah say, mister, isn't that t' sun?"

The other chimed in: "Nay, it's mooin, isn't it?"

Not wishing to be involved, he replied: "Well, to tell yer t' truth, Ah'm a stranger i' theeas parts."

Scene: Settle market place. Two elderly men, sat on a seat, are approached by a hiker.

"Can you tell me the shortest way to Kirkby Lonsdale?"

One of the men looked blankly at the other and said: "Nay, Ah doan't knaw."

But the other one spoke up brightly: "Well," he said. "If I wanted to goa t' shortest way, Ah wodn't start thru 'ere."

An American tourist called one evening at a remote Dales public house, to find he was the sole customer.

After a while though another man came in at the door, walked up the wall, across the ceiling, down the other wall, and then ordered a pint.

After drinking his pint, he returned by the same method – up the wall, across the ceiling, and down the other wall and so out into the night.

The American said to the barman: "Gee. That guy's odd."

The Dales barman replied: "Tha mustn't think nowt about it. He nivver sez goodneet."

A clergyman from the Home Counties was on a walking tour in Cleveland. As he was going along Thimbleby Way, he encountered an elderly local sweeping up leaves with a besom.

"How long will it take me to reach Swainby, my man?" inquired the cleric.

The old man made no reply so the reverend repeated the question in louder tones with the same result. Not a flicker of comprehension passed over the old man's features.

So thinking he had had the misfortune to meet a deaf mute, the parson began to walk away, but before he had gone many yards, a loud clear voice called out: "It'll tak tha two hours."

"Then why couldn't you say so before?" said the now very angry minister.

"Nay, I nobbut wanted to see how fast tha could walk."

Two farmer's lads, one of whom was having his annual holiday, were talking:

"Has ta bin anywheear for thi holidays?"

"Aye, Ah went ta Skipt'n a Munda', Starbott'n a Tuesda', Kilsa' Show Wensda, Starbott'n ageean a Thursda', an' naa Ah'm off ta Skipt'n ageean a Frida'."

"By lad, tha's travelled, 'en't ta?" said the other, in tones of unfeigned awe.

A jewellery collector entered an antique shop in a Dales village to have a look round. A young girl stood behind the counter. In front of her on a piece of paper rested what looked like a round yellow marble. The collector noticed it.

"That," he said excitedly, "is either a wonderful topaz or an exceptionally rare piece of amber. Where did you get it?"

"Nay," retorted the girl. "That's me bit of barley sugar I've just been sucking."

Many years ago a Yank was touring Britain in his Cadillac. Being lost he stopped to enquire his whereabouts of the road-sweeper.

Yank: "Say boy, what's the name of this place?"

Sweeper: "This is Cleckheaton, Yorkshire, sir."

Yank: "My word, this sure is a one horse town."

Sweeper: "You wouldn't think so mate, if you had my job."

A French girl had married a British soldier at the end of the First World War, and came to settle with him in a small town in Yorkshire. She always retained a strong French accent but acquired a considerable grasp of the local idiom.

When her husband's health was failing, she and her son took on the job of cleaning the church hall, with satisfactory results. She told a neighbour: "Ze kitchen is far bettair now. Before it vos, 'ow you say, mucky as owt."

Wishing to do the right thing, an American motorist stopped to square matters with a North Riding farmer whose cockerel he had hit.

"Pardon me," said the motorist. "I killed your rooster with my car. I've come to let you know I'm willing to replace him."

"Hm," answered the farmer, "well, let's hear you crow."

During the war a Belgian refugee aged about fifteen years went to stay on a Yorkshire farm. The farmer was supposed to keep him employed with work – light jobs and so forth.

One day he sent the boy to gather all the sheep from the home pasture and bring them to the yard. As the dogs didn't understand the boy's lingo they wouldn't go with him to help. But off he went in high glee. After a long time, he arrived with them eventually and the farmer asked. "Had some trouble with them?"

"Yes," replied the Belgian. "The white ones [sheep] came easy but that brown one [a hare] took some rounding up."

A young man from the city thought he would like a country job for a change, and went to call on a farmer on the North Yorkshire Moors.

"Well," said the farmer. "I don't know what a city man could do here. Do you think you could shoe a horse?"

"Well," said the man. "I'm willing to try."

"All right, I've got to go into the village for an hour or so. See what you can make of the job."

When the farmer returned he found the horse lying on its back, with all four feet stuck up in the air. It had been shod, though, and the job had been well done.

"You've made a good fist of that," he complimented. "But what's the matter with the horse? He looks a bit odd."

"I've been worrying about that," replied the young man. "He's been like that ever since I took him out of the vice."

A visitor to a small fishing village on the East Yorkshire coast was heard to remark to one of the locals: "Whatever do you find to do down here during the winter?"

To which came the blunt reply: "T'same as i' summer, but wi' us owercoats on."

An amateur artist was painting in Dent when a shower of rain induced him to take refuge in a large opening next to a public house. As he was completing the painting, up came a village elder, who looked at the work, then said:

"By gum, lad, that's all reight. I'll tell thee what, when tha's done it tha wants to tak it into pub tha'll get a fiver for it. I've sin 'em give a fiver for a lot worse na that."

At a mining town in New Zealand, Yorky had played his concertina at a local concert. While waiting to enter the mine next morning, Scotty, a local piper, tried to take a rise out of him.

"Och, yer bletherin' auld concertina. Yer hev tae hang out the bedroom window so's ye'll hae all the street tae swing it in."

"Well, lad," replied Yorky. "Maybe tha's reet, but Ah doan't hev ter tak me trousers off ter play it."

An exceptionally silky miniature Yorkshire Terrier was sitting up like a statue on the back shelf of a three-wheel bubble car.

As it waited at traffic lights an astonished American voice could be heard to exclaim: "Well. Whaddya know – a long-haired chihuahua."

An American visitor to Harrogate was boasting to a local about his country. "For example," he said. "You can ride in one train all day and never leave the county you started in."

His companion nodded. "Yes, we have the same trouble with our trains," he said.

"Keep yer hands in yer pocket, lad…unless yer lose t' toss."

During the last war a German plane was shot down, crashing in a field near a village in Holderness. A shocked and bleeding crew member crawled out of the wrecked plane, to be confronted by a grim looking Yorkshire farmhand.

The German indicated he was wounded, hoping for some sympathy.

The response was pointed and brief. The farmer replied (in broad East Riding dialect): "Well, tho shun't a cum."

A Yorkshireman had been invited to spend a week with a friend in London. Off he went, and the week lengthened into a fortnight. At the end of that period, the Tyke decided to return to his native county.

The London friend went to the station to see his guest off and on arrival there they decided to have one last drink together. As they entered the buffet, the Londoner put his hand into his pocket to pay for the drinks.

"Sithee 'ere, owd lad," said the Yorkshireman. "Tha's been good enough to keep mi' an' pay for all mi' drinks this last fortneet, an' Ah think it's time Ah did summat. Ah'll tell thee wot we'll do – we'll toss for it."

In Leeds the Polyglot Society has many European members with now amusing (but then highly embarrassing) anecdotes of their first attempts to adapt to our language and customs amidst Yorkshire folk.

One charming Italian lady tells of her attempts to be polite, courteous and correct as a young woman first arriving in Leeds and invited to a meal.

Very concerned as to how one used the word 'breast' in company, she demurely asked, looking at the chicken on the table: "Just a little of the bosom, please."

But she really must have floored the assembly as, feeling warm, she announced: "I'm prostituted with the heat."

A Southern woman became a teacher at a school near Bradford. On the first day she accumulated a quantity of rubbish and left her classroom in search of the dustbin. One of the masters was returning from the direction of the gate. "Where's the bin?" she enquired. "Ah've bin t' Bull if it's owt to do wi' thee," came the blunt reply.

In a certain hostelry at Whitsuntide an 'off-cumed un' was laying down the law about the lack of enterprise in rural areas. He thought Dales folk were a 'queer lot' and ended by asking one old chap what he did all winter.

The old chap looked thoughtful, and then said: "Well, after t' day's work we make up a good fire – and then we talk about all t' queer folk who've been here during t' summer."

A Yorkshireman, who for many years lived part of each year in Suffolk, was once asked by a local clergyman: "What is the difference between Yorkshire people and Suffolk people?"

"Well," replied the Yorkshireman. "When you call and see Yorkshire people in their homes, they put the kettle on, but in Suffolk they take it off."

Having journeyed to Dent on a tour of the Dales, the Londoner sat in the local and talked with the villagers.

"What a pull up your hill to the station," he said. "I wonder why they built it there."

"Well," said wise old John, "I reckon it was because they wanted it near t' lines."

An elderly Yorkshireman was spending a holiday in London. He was sitting in the entrance lounge of his hotel when another guest entered and asked the old man if he had seen his wife come in. Being a Southerner, he was rather baffled when the Yorkshireman replied: "Aye, shoo's just gone up in th'oist."

An American couple were doing a tour of York Minster. The man said irritably: "Let's get a move on. How do you think we're going to see York if you keep stopping to look at things?"

In the old days, 'trips' to London were run by the old NER, and passengers getting into the train from small places in Wensleydale joined the London train at Northallerton.

One old man from Hawes paid his first visit to London in this way, and stood outside the Mansion House watching the traffic.

A policeman said to him "Busy, isn't it?"

To which the old man replied:

"Aye. There's a trip fra 'Awes in."

Said a Londonder to an old villager in his cottage on the cliff top at Kettleness: "There cannot be much fresh air in these old places."

"Young man," replied the native. "There's more fresh air comes through our keyhole than you have in all London."

Old Walter was leaning on a field gate listening to a rather flashy couple from London bent on impressing Walter of their importance.

Walter had tried to put up with this, but found at last he could stand no more of their swank, so when they asked him if he had ever been up to London to see the sights, Walter calmly replied: "No, I haven't, but now and agean sights come up here to look at me."

A Scotsman married a Yorkshire woman, and they set up house in Yorkshire. Two sons were born.

"They're half Yorkshire and half Scots," their father told a friend. "They're thrifty lads. They can save. That's Scots. But it's my money they save. That's Yorkshire."

A man moved from London to Yorkshire and decided to take up farming. He went off to the supplier near his new small-holding and said to the assistant: "100 baby chickens, please." The assistant duly produced 100 chicks.

A week later the man was back, and said to the same assistant: "I'd like 200 baby chickens please."

The assistant complied.

A further week later, the man was back again. This time he asked: "Please may I have 500 baby chickens?"

"Goodness," the assistant replied. "You must be doing well."

"Well, not really," said the man, looking perplexed. "I can't quite work it out yet, but I reckon I'm either planting them too deep or too far apart."

A Southerner on holiday in Swaledale frequented the village inn. Here his curiosity was aroused by a three-foot-six-inch man with a cauliflower ear and an insatiable thirst for ale.

On the last day of his holiday, the visitor made inquiries into the background of this local character. "That man used to be six feet tall," explained the landlord. "His unselfish hero-ism saved eighty men in a leadmine accident. He managed to hold up the roof with his head while his mates scrambled out."

"But how did he get the cauliflower ear?" asked the tourist. "Well," said the landlord, "we had the devil of a job knocking him into place with a shovel."

The Yorkshireman exiled in London found that the Cockneys he worked with were always taking the mickey out of his accent. The final straw came when one proclaimed: "They're all a bit fick up norf ain't they?"

After a pause the Yorkshireman replied thoughtfully: "Nay I don't knaw so much abaht that. I wor allus taught 'as dens-est population wor in London."

A Yorkshire farmer went to see the sights of London and, feeling in need of refreshment, went into a restaurant for a meal.

He had to sit with three other men at the table and, as was his home custom, said his grace before starting to eat.

He saw the other men making fun and on his inquiring what the joke was about, they said: "Well, we don't say grace before meals."

To which the Yorkshireman replied: "Neither do the pigs back on my farm."

The venue was London and the occasion the Sedbergh Tradesmen's holiday. Mr A had a daughter, Elsie, living in London, and as he was passing along the street he was greeted by Mrs F with the comment: "My, it will be nice for your Elsie in London today."

"Why?" asked Mr A.

"Well, she'll be sure to run across some o't Sebber folk i't main street."

Overheard in the Calcutta Light Horse Club:

"Ah suppose tha'll be going ter the Lancashire and Cheshire Do."

"Noa lad, Ah've nowt ter do wi' foreigners. Ah coom fra Yorkshire."

Four South Country friends enjoyed a day out in the Dales. At the end of it they stopped at an inn for a drink, and asked the woman who was serving for one bitter, two milds and one mixed. She noted the order carefully and left.

A few minutes later she was back with the four glasses which she put on one table. When asked which was which she said to them:

"Nay, thi mun choose for thissens. They're all out o' t' same tub."

While visiting his son in London a Dales farmer noticed four road labourers taking a breather, leaning on their shovels.

"Typical Southerners," he growled. "Three doin' nowt an' one helpin' 'em."

A party of Southerners on a coach trip round Yorkshire saw a windmill for the first time. They asked a local what on earth that thing with the sails was.

"Nay, doa't tha knaw?" he said. "That's an electric fan to keep t' cows cool."

It took place in Piccadilly, Manchester, while Bryan was waiting for some friends to join him in an outing to the cricket match at Old Trafford. The day, Whit Monday; processions all over the place; and men with boxes of red roses propped up against statues of them long dead. On approaching one of these vendors he asked: "Have you got a white rose, please?"

"No," was the reply. There was a pause, and then:

"D'you come thro' Yorkshire?"

"Yes."

The vendor immediately commented: "No, we nobbut use white roses for wreaths over 'ere."

Mary, a cousin from over the Pennines, was helping in the village shop when an old man came in.

"Ah want sum peas," he said.

Mary offered him a tin of peas.

"No, no, peas," he insisted.

"Do you mean dried peas?" asked Mary.

"No. Sum o' them theer," said the old man in exasperation, pointing to some tins of pears on the shelf.

The puzzled expression left Mary's face.

"Oh, you mean purs," she said, as handed him the tin.

Tom was born this side of Oldham, at Springhead; and that makes him a Yorkshireman. But his twang at the time could have misled anybody into thinking that he was a 'Lanky'. When he left the village for a Midlands town years ago, his twang was noticed by the Lancastrians of the place; and they invited him to join their society.

"But I'm a Yorkshireman," he protested.

"It doesn't matter," came the reply. "You talk like one of us. Besides, t' treasurer's job's open and we've nobody we can trust wi' t' brass."

A passenger in a very full railway compartment made the extraordinary boast that he could tell a man's county of origin merely from his looks – he did not need to hear him speak. He readily accepted the challenge of his sceptical fellow travellers to justify his incredible boast.

One after the other he went round the compartment. At some he paused a little longer than at others, but one by one he identified their county of origin at the first attempt.

Finally, he came to the last man – a big fourteen-stone fellow sitting in a corner seat. He glanced at him only briefly, then said with absolute assurance.

"Well, well, there's no mistaking you, my friend. You're a Lancastrian, aren't you?"

The man looked a little offended as he replied, with some irritation:

"Nay, tha's wrong this time, lad, Ah'm a Yorkshireman. But Ah've not been very well recently."

An off-cumed un was pontificating in a pub near Grassington.

"Remember what William Shakespeare said – 'All's well that ends well.' "

"Shakespeare, eh?" replied a local. "He must've come from t' Dales 'cos we've been saying that for years."

An expatriate Yorkshireman now living in Staffordshire was told by friends there that he still had a broad West Riding accent. Secure in the knowledge, therefore, that he was easily recognisable as from the county of Broad Acres, imagine his chagrin when the following incident occurred:

On a visit to Birmingham he was asked for directions. On replying, in his native tongue, that as a visitor himself he was unable to help, back came the muttered reply:

"Those bl--dy Lancastrians."

Harry was introduced to a Lancashire lad. As he took Harry's hand he said: "Tha's from Yorkshire, eh?"

"Aye, lad," he replied.

"'Ere," he said, "give us t' other hand as well. Last Yorkshireman Ah shook hands with picked me pocket."

A motorist travelling a country road was anxious to speed rather than loiter. A flock of sheep was being moved from one pen to another, and the motorist got entangled. His progress was reduced almost to a standstill.

There were one or two men accompanying the sheep, and he was not sure who to address regarding the hold-up. In desperation he shouted: "Who is the master of these sheep?" The answer came from a burly shepherd: "That little black faced 'un i' t' front."

Many years ago two city dwellers on a cycling tour in North Yorkshire decided to spend a night at a wayside inn. After a meal the landlord suggested they had a game of billiards, and took them into a tiny room with a crazy-looking little table and a set of balls all of a dull grey colour. This rather puzzled the two men, and one asked the landlord: "How do you tell the red from the white?"

"That's easy," he said. "By their shape."

"Don't blame me, blame the leader."

A retired City banker, an off-cumed un, who had just moved into the village manor house, inveigled his way onto the parish council. Full of newly elected zeal, he bought a book about parochial responsibilities. Having discovered that these included the preservation of old footpaths, he suggested at the first meeting that this subject should be put on the agenda as a matter of urgency. Reluctantly, this was agreed.

At the second meeting, the parish clerk solemnly produced a fifty-year-old map of the parish, on which was highlighted a footpath starting from the main road near the manor house – and passing straight across what was now the retired banker's tennis court.

Dent is famed for the longevity of its natives. An American walking through the village noticed a man of over seventy sitting crying on a door step.

"Say, boy," he asked. "What's wrong?"

"Mi fadder's just gen mi a good hidin' fer thraa'n steans at mi gran'fadder," was the reply.

TALKING TYKE

*learning the language – lost in translation –
Yorkshire yammer*

Reyt. We need to get summat straight befoor wi gu any
further. T' one thing that stops thi appreciating Yorkshire
dialect on't page is that punctuation mark I've just put
between n and t of on't. I'm referring of course to t' curse of
all writers of vernacular speech, t' apostrophe. T' flippin apostrophe in all its subtlety and ethereal gorgeousness and poten-
tial misuse. T' apostrophe: the umlaut of the Dales!

You can see from the above paragraph how difficult it is to
render the beauty and variety of Yorkshire language in written
form; know-nowt Southern types think they're being oh so
accurate when they write a phrase like 'trubble at't mill'; well,
I've got news for those people: nobody has ever, outside the
pages of novels written about Yorkshire by people who've
never been north of Crewe, put that intrusive 't' in front of the
apostrophe. As we know, it's not 'Trubble at't mill' it's (and
here I wish I could be by your side, whispering in your ear,
whoever you are) 'Trubble at' mill'. There's no T. The little
sliver of white space after the apostrophe and before the M of
mill denotes a tiny gap in the universe, a silence in the music
of the spheres. It's a little packet of nothingness that a lot of
the rhythms of Yorkshire dialect are built around and under
and through.

"I'm going to' shop. I'm getting eggs and flour." No intrusive T, my friends, no intrusive T. Of course, if you slip over
the border (accidentally, of course) to Lancashire, then you

get the full intrusive 'th' as in "I'm taking th' animals to th' abbatoir!" but such intrusions needn't concern us. They're just th' height o' daftness.

So this chapter is full of cracking humour in Yorkshire dialect and it's all funny but remember that dialect is mainly an oral form rather than a written one. Yorkshire language is a tapestry made of sounds that constantly change and soften and harden as bits drop off and bits are added and new words are coined until they run out of usefulness and then they're dropped. In Barnsley we say 'now then thee', but in Sheffield, just fifteen miles down the road, they say 'nar den dee'. Then up the M1 in Bradford they've lost their T and often their G, and the apostrophe comes into its own as they say It's a bi' of a be'ar when you've go' a go a Ba'ley, and then in North Yorkshire they gang yam frum Yark races.

Enjoy this chapter, and if you run out of apostrophes, here's a few to keep you going:'''

Ian McMillan

Dougie asked his brother how his nephew, who is an agricultural student, was coming along with his studies.

His father said: "Well, tha knows, he still ploughs t' same way, but he talks different. He allus used to say: 'Whoa Ned,' when he gat to th' end ot' furrow and then it was: 'Gee up, lad.' Now he's that posh he says: 'Halt, Edward. Pivot and proceed.' T' horse can't understand him. So I'm telling you, it's no good sending anybody away to learn farming unless tha sends t' horse an' all."

Two Yorkshiremen, Bill and Tom, were in a lodging house. Bill gave Tom a sheep's head to boil. Tom did so but let it boil dry. Bill returned to find Tom kicking the sheep's head around the room, saying: "The ruddy thing's supped all t' broth."

A pupil had been off school with ear trouble. On his return the headmaster asked him: "Is your ear better now?"

Pupil: "Eh?"

HM: "Your ear – is it any better?"

Pupil: "Eh?"

HM (shouting, almost): "How's your ear?"

Pupil: "Eh?"

HM (exasperated): "Ors thi lug 'ot thee, lad?"

Pupil: "Oh no, it's better now."

Overheard in a Leeds bus: "My sister and me," said a woman, "we ain't no more alike than if we wasn't us. Yes, she's just as different as me, only the other way."

A Dales schoolteacher was correcting a boy who had said: "I ain't going to go there."

"That is not the right way to talk," she said. "Listen: I am not going there; thou art not going there; he is not going there; we are not going there; you are not going there; they are not going there. Now, do you understand?"

"Yes, miss. There ain't nobody going."

A very stout mother arrived at the head teacher's office on the second floor of a large city school in Sheffield one day, so out of breath from the exertion of climbing the stairs that for a short time she was completely speechless. The headmistress waited until she had recovered her breath, and then asked what she could do for her.

"Ah've come to say ahr Mary won't be at schooil to-day, 'cos she's got diarrhoea."

The headmistress thanked her for calling, but pointed out that she could have sent a note instead. The mother's reply was brief but forthright: "Does ta think Ah'd 'ave climbed all your bloomin' stairs if Ah could 'ave spelt that word?"

"Are you under t' doctor yet?"

"Aye."

"What sort o' tablets is ta takkin'?"

"White uns. What's thine like?"

"White uns."

"What do the' call 'em?"

" 'Asbefore'."

"Oh, mine isn't same – mine's called 'Asdirected'."

Two locals were discussing a mutual friend who had lost much weight. "He's that thin now," said one, "he's like a owporth o' sooap after a lang day's wesh."

Mark visited one of Yorkshire's open gardens and stopped to talk to an aged gardener at work there. He congratulated him on his vigour.

"Aye," he said. "Ah've been man and boy in this 'ere garden five and sixty year, and still does my eight hour a day. Not so bad for an octogeranium, is it?"

At a Yorkshire stately home which was open to the public a real old-fashioned Tyke was in charge of the gardens. When visitors saw his roses and dahlias they would ask him how he grew such large blooms. His answer was: "Manure, plenty of manure." Then when visitors saw his vegetable garden they would ask: "How do you grow such large turnips and cabbages?" His answer, as always, was: "Manure, plenty of manure."

One day his wife and grown-up daughter were standing near when the old man was talking to visitors. The daughter said to her mother: "I wish dad would say 'fertiliser' to the visitors instead of 'manure'."

Mother turned round to the daughter and said: "You leave your father alone. It took me twenty years to get him to say manure."

Two small boys stood looking up at the statue of Sir Titus Salt in Manningham Park. One of them read out the title inscribed underneath: "Sir Titus Salt, Bart."

Turning to the other one he said: "What does 'Bart' mean?"

The other one looked up at the statue again and replied: "Why, baht 'at, of course."

An old Yorkshireman wandered slowly home from a visit to the doctors with the verdict of his consultation sitting heavily on his mind. On reaching home he found his wife busy working upstairs. Going to the foot of the stairs he called out: "I say, lass, I'm bahn to 'ev an appendectomy."

Quickly the retort came from above: "Tha's heving nowt till 'have 'ed mi new 'at."

A coach party of shop assistants from York on a day trip entered a pub in the North York Moors.

The only other customers in the pub when the party entered were two farm hands who heard themselves described as 'country bumpkins' by some of the party. One of them said to the other in a very loud voice:

"Tak nea notice o' them, they're nobbut a lot o' counter jumpers oot o' Yorrk. They can't measure a yard o' lastic wi'oot stretching it."

A group of schoolboys were discussing their English literature homework on a Huddersfield bus.

One muttered: "Stand not upon the order of your going," whereupon a distinguished-looking gentleman sitting behind him leaned forward and asked the lad if he could tell him the meaning of the quotation.

For a moment the boy looked puzzled, then, his face clearing, he answered: "Yus, it mee-ans 'be sharp and b----r off' i' Shay-ekspeare."

The new recruits were lined up on the barrack square. The colonel shouted: "All officers to the front," and a little private, a native of Ossett, stepped out smartly.

"What's the matter with you, my man?" cried the colonel.

"Well, sir," replied the private. "You said you wanted all t' Ossetters to t' front."

Freda and Joe decided to go to a 'posh' place for lunch. The soup arrived, very hot, and Joe started blowing it noisily.

"Nay Joah, tha doesn't do that in posh spots lahke this."

"Wat mun I do then? It's too hot to sup."

"Tha mun waft it with thi cap."

The pronunciation of the word 'bath' has always been a source of dispute between North and South. The other day a Yorkshireman was discovered giving the word a southern touch. It became 'barth'.

A young man from the South, now resident in Yorkshire, was asked what he called it. He wasn't sure. "You see," he explained, "the people I'm living with have got me into the way of calling it a 'wash-all-over'."

Old Sam travelled to town on the early bus, and often sat next to a seventy-year-old who had a mile ride to help with morning chores in the local.

The other day Sam had need to use the same bus. His friend and he exchanged greetings once more. He observed: "Ah ain't seen thee lately. Ez tha been inebriatin' for t' winter?"

A Daleswoman was comparing prices and quality at a market stall in a Dales town when the stallholder asked if he could help her.

"Nay," she said, "Ahberrerlerrergerremersen." (And that is not one of those Welsh railway station names.)

A man had difficulties with restrictions and materials when building his bungalow after the war. He appropriately gave it the grand name of 'Mun-do'.

Woman of a neighbour who nags her husband: "She takes somethin' that dun't amount to nowt, an' then she ovvers an' ovvers it."

"Father, what does e-i-t-h-e-r spell?" asked young Bob one night as he sat reading his spelling book.

"Well," replied his father. "Some fowk call it eyther, an' some fowk call it eether, so it seems to me tha'll be reight if tha calls it awther."

Yorkshire phrase indicating a chap in a hurry: "If he were cawd, he'd not hev time ter shiver."

The vicar was inspecting a Dales school on scripture.

"What does it mean where we read of Our Lord 'And they were astonished at His Doctrine'?" he asked.

Up went a quick hand. "Please sir," said one of the scholars. "They were fair capped."

A Londoner who did not know the Yorkshire dialect was asked to visit a friend who lived in one of the Dales villages. His host knew the village schoolmaster who invited him to go along to the school and ask the scholars in one of the classes a few questions.

"Now," said the guest, "I will give £1 to the boy who answers my question correctly. Who was it who went into the ark with the animals?"

He pointed to a smart little boy and said: "Do you know who went into the ark with the animals?"

"Noa," said the lad. He duly received £1.

A Dales farmer went to a Yorkshire show.

"How did yo like it?" someone asked.

The farmer scratched his head. "Well, if Ah wor goin' agean, I wouldn't go," he said.

A self-made man who possessed his own works petrol pump found his Rolls Royce was out of fuel. He visited a country petrol station. The garage man approached the car with pleasant anticipation of supplying ten gallons or more. On being asked for half a gallon, his instant reponse was: "What's tha doing, weaning it?"

Many years ago, a Yorkshire lady rang her merchant to order a supply of coal and asked for an early delivery, adding "S'il vous plaît."

The coal merchant asked her what she meant by this. She explained that, as we were newly in the Common Market, we must practise our French and she was trying it out.

"Oh, in that case madam," said the merchant, "how would you like it – cul de sac or à la carte?"

During the last war in a unit of Royal Marines were two 'Yorkies'. One who spoke good English acted as interpreter to the other who spoke a rich Dewsbury dialect.

One day when 'Dewsbury' had been giving voice, a listener said: "Hey Yorkie, if you call a hole an 'oil, what do you say for oil?"

Like lightning came the answer "Grease."

Two women were looking at the meat on display in a butcher's shop. The prices were large and the joints of meat small. One woman said to the other:

"Fancy, £2 for that bit. When you gorrit cooked it'd nobbut look like another crack in t' meat dish."

Betty was employed in a 'posh' town for a number of years and rather lost her Yorkshire speech. Sometime later she took a job in the village shop. One day a customer ordered a rabbit to be skinned and jointed ready for cooking. As Bettty could not do this, she asked her to leave it until the 'boss' came back.

On giving him her instructions, he asked: "Does shoo want it livering?"

Betty replied: "Oh, she didn't mention its liver."

Whereupon he said: "I mean is shoo barn to foitch it, or 'ev I to take it round to her 'ouse?"

A Barnsley man was so fond of his Yorkshire terrier that when it died he took it to a taxidermist and asked him to stuff and then gold-plate his pet as a permanent memorial.

"Eighteen carats?" asked the taxidermist.

"No," the man replied, "chewing a bone."

On a tour of Wales, the driver stopped the coach as they skirted the base of Snowdon.

He waxed very poetical, pointing upwards: "Look you, people, is it not a wonderful sight?"

A sceptical Yorkshireman said grudgingly: "Aye, but when all's said an' done, lad, it's nowt but a gert lump o' muck."

Old Enoch was a character who lived in a Dales village with his ailing wife. He was usually to be found sitting near the cottage door making odds and ends out of timber he found round about the village.

One day, when the doctor called, Enoch was hammering some pieces of wood.

"How is your wife today?" asked the doctor.

"Oh pretty bad, sir, pretty bad."

"Is that her coughing?"

"Oh no," said Enoch, "this is a chicken coop."

Heard in York market: "Nay, Ah don't lik them quiet chaps as say nowt. As mi old father used to warn me, it's t' quietest pig as eats most o' t' food i' trough."

It was Christmas Eve in a North Yorkshire village. Snowflakes whirled as the villagers plodded cheerfully, in twos and threes, down the street towards the gleaming lights of the village hall. A visitor asked: "What's going on?"

"Oh," replied an elderly lady eagerly, "our WI's givin' yan o' these 'ere activity plays."

In a Dales village an evening class was studying German.

"Now," said the German-born teacher. "Tonight, ve vill talk about a railvay journey: ve vill start on ze station. Ze German for railvay station is 'der Bahnhof'. Can anybody find a gut vay to remember der Bahnhof?"

"Aye, lad, Ah can," said a voice.

Everyone gasped. It was the dunce of the class who had answered.

"Oh yes, Mr X, and just how vill you remember zis word Bahnhof?"

"Well," said the student, "whenever Ah go to t' station Ah'm allus bahn off somewheer."

The teacher never understood why the whole class roared with laughter.

A Yorkshireman visiting London one hot day, decided to freshen up at the public baths, so asked a passer-by to direct him.

"Yus mate," said the man. "Do you want the big bas or the little bas? The little bas goes from here, and the double-decker across the road."

The Yorkshireman looked puzzled, then said: "It's the baths I want, where I can get washed."

"Oh," said the Cockney. "You mean the barths."

"That tractor thoo selled me's a bad 'un. Will tha tak it back?"

"Not likely; thoo should ha' found out afore tho bought it."

"Then I'll tak tha ti court."

"Please thisen but thoo knows what t' judge'll say."

"What?"

"He'll say, 'Caveat emptor'."

"And what does that mean?"

"It means thoo's had it."

At the chapel in Horton-in-Ribblesdale, the preacher, a local farmer cum lay-reader, was telling the parable of the Prodigal Son. To emphasise his story, he made a sweeping gesture with an arm saying:

"Sithee, fowks, ye mon picture him coming over Peny-ghent, bare heead, bare foot, wi' his breeches arse out."

"Ah made a reight grahnd meyt pie," complained Mum, "and all your dad did, wah sit dahn and eyt it."

Abe was notorious for his dissolute lifestyle.

"For a long time," he said to a friend, "I was ashamed of the way I lived my life."

"You mean you reformed?"

"No, I got ovver being ashamed."

A southern gentleman was producing a show in a small Yorkshire town in aid of charity a few years back.

It was necessary for one of the scenes to have a carpet, so he went to a nearby furnishing shop to enquire if, in the cause of charity, they would loan him one for use in the play. They were very pleased to do so. Wishing to make it safe for the actors he asked: "May I tack it?"

"There's no need," was the reply. "We'll send it round to you later today."

Two youngsters were playing 'I Spy'.

Billy (a true Yorkshireman) said "T," and Tommy (from Essex) after guessing "Table," "Teaspoon," etc gave up.

Triumphantly Billy said "T' oven door."

After giving a lesson on buildings to a class in a Yorkshire school, the teacher, seeing that Johnny hadn't been paying much attention, asked him if he could give three different examples of types of windows usually found in houses.

After quick thought, Johnny replied: "Yes, sir. Oppun, shut and brokkun."

A doctor was called to a family for the first time, and not getting very bright or helpful replies to his queries asked mother what her husband died of. She pondered and then said brightly: "He died of a Wednesday."

A school party had been into the village on a coach trip, and the talk in the local turned to modern life and education.

"Nay," said one old fellow in the corner, as he leaned over to a man who could have been forty years younger. "We make nowt of eddication up here, lad. We just uses our brains instead."

The mill foreman was not impressed with the performance of his new employee: "If he moved any slower he'd be doin' yesterday's work."

Old Bob was being carried to his last resting place up the short but steep church path by his old cronies. As the day was hot and sultry, a halt had to be called halfway.

"Let's fetch the bier," said old Tom.

"Aye," said old Ned. "Nowt would ev pleased Bob better than to think that he was being put away with a pint."

One East Riding lady to another: "Aye, an' I said to 'is mother, 'He'll never die as long as he lives.' "

A loquacious witness in a Leeds court was told by the magistrate to be a little more terse in his evidence.

"I suppose you know what terse means."

"Of course I do. It's t' first coach at a funeral."

In the period between the two world wars, an urban district council in South Yorkshire had proudly completed its first council housing estate, and the housing committee sat in solemn conclave, trying to find a name for it.

"That's easy," said one of the members. "Ah reckon that we owt ter cal 'em T' Cloisters."

"Cloisters?" exclaimed the others, mystified.

"Aye, because they're clois ter t' shops, they're clois ter t' pub, they're clois ter t' cinema, they're clois ter t' church, they're clois ter t' cemetry. They're clois ter ivverything."

Two scholars watched the headmaster write an address and, puzzling about the word 'Lancs', were told to think what 'Yorks' stood for.

"Ah," beamed one. "I know, sir – them things in eggs."

"When I was little we had a dog called Grieg, after t' composer, like."

"That's odd. Did it like classical music or summat?"

"No, it used to pee agin t' suite."

THE LAST WORD

there's no answer to that –
funerals and wakes – clever clogs

In the village where I live, in the heart of the old South Yorkshire coalfield, there's a grave just in the shadow of the imposing tower.

'Here lies the body of John Smith' it reads (I'm changing the name because it's odds on his ancestors will be *Dalesman* readers) 'who inadvertently pulled this stone upon himself whilst in the service of his master'.

Now that's what I call a memorial inscription. In fact, now that's what I call a Yorkshire Memorial Inscription! (and wouldn't that make a great series? Better than *Now That's What I Call Music 994*, or whichever number they're onto now).

Just picture the scene.

It's young John's first day at work and he's eager to please the master, who is imposing in breeches and a cap. The master asks John just to unload an impossibly huge stone from the back of the car. The master doesn't use the phrase 'impossibly huge' of course. John attempts to lift it, totters, staggers, slips and is crushed like a cartoon character. The rest of the workers look on in horror but the master just snaps his fingers and says "Just dig a hole and bury him under the stone..."

Memorials and inscriptions and funerals and funeral teas ("We buried him with ham") are part of the Yorkshire Life Cycle, which is a bit like those old cycles the Co-op boys used to deliver on: wobbly and potentially lethal. At my mother's funeral the pall bearers were older than her and they all had combovers and it was a windy day and so walking to the chapel from the hearse was like walking through a lagoon of grey seaweed, and maybe that's what the best funerals are: a mixture of the tragic and the comic. My mother would have laughed, anyway.

This final chapter isn't just about the Final Chapter, if you get my drift. It's also about the Last Word, the way that Yorkshire folks won't ever let anybody have the ultimate say in a conversation. You have a look, next time you're out and about in Yorkshire; you'll see a couple of folk kallin' as they say round these parts. They'll appear to have finished their conversation, then one will say something. The other will turn as if to go and then they'll reply. The first will pause and then will say a word. The other will almost look defeated but will then produce a phrase from the air. And so it will go on. If you go back later on to get your evening paper they'll still be there, still doing the conversation dance, still hoping for the last word, neither one willing to admit defeat, and in the course of their kallathon they'll have said some pretty ridiculous things, like the ones you'll find if you turn the page.

Go on, turn it.

Go on.

I've finished.

I'm telling you, I've finished.

Done.

Nowt to say.

Nowt.

Ian McMillan

On his parish round of visits, the vicar called on a local farmer who was a born pessimist.

"I'm glad to know your wife is better," began the vicar brightly.

"You wouldn't be if you 'ad to live with 'er," complained the farmer.

"You have a nice garden here," was the vicar's next effort.

"None so bad for 'em as don't have to dig in it."

"You seem to have a good supply of water."

"Maybe, but it's all to be pumped."

The vicar played his last card. "Well, it's nice weather, at any rate."

"Yes, for 'em as ain't nothin' to do but enjoy it," was the final rejoinder.

A Hawes man called on an elderly neighbour to tell him a mutual friend had gone to hospital to have a leg amputated.

"Nay, you don't say," the neighbour declared. "D'ye mean his foot and all?"

The visitor rang the front door bell and asked whether Mr Smith was at home.

"Which Mr Smith?" asked the maid. "There are two brothers living here."

The visitor thought for a moment. Then his face brightened.

"Why, of course," he said eagerly. "The one who has a sister living in Bradford."

Mike was lost in Cleveland while trying to find a secondary school. He inquired from an old man where the school might be, to be told: "Tha's never going to that school."

"Why, do you know the place?"

"Know it?" he laughed. "I'm the rear gunner on the school meals van."

Old Mary never beat about the bush. Dissatisfied with the quality of the milk that she fetched each morning from a neighbouring farm, she took two jugs one day instead of one.

"Ah'll hev milk i' woon an' watter in t' oother," she explained, "an' mix mi own."

The oldest inhabitant of a West Riding village had reached his hundredth birthday, and the local paper sent a reporter along to visit him.

"To what do you attribute your long life?" asked the reporter.

"To the fact that I was born so long ago," replied the old man.

There was something of a scare in a North Country town owing to a slight epidemic of smallpox, and many people were being vaccinated as a precautionary measure.

The local doctor, finding that his rooms were inadequate to deal with the increased number of patients, took the kitchen underneath and had it converted into a temporary surgery.

"I'm afraid," said the nurse, glancing round the crowded room, "that some of you will have to be vaccinated in the basement."

"Not on your life," replied a navvy. "I'll be vaccinated on the arm, or not at all."

Two Yorkshiremen found themselves travelling in the same compartment on a train. Neither spoke for a while, but eventually the first one said: "Thou's an ugly looking fellow."

The other one replied: "Can I help what I look like?"

"No," said the first one, "but thou cud 'ave stopped at home."

When an old Wolds farmer was told by his doctor to have a simpler diet, he objected strongly. "Aw'm nut gooing to starve mysen to death for t' sake o' living a few years longer."

A Rydale man had bought a new overcoat and brought it home for inspection.

"It looks all right," said his wife, "but it seems queer when you put it on."

The new owner looked at himself in a mirror. "It's that fool of a tailor," he said. "He's put a button short at the bottom and one too many at the top."

In a café in an East Riding market town a facetious customer asked for a piece of toast, an egg, a cup of coffee and a kind word. The order was duly executed, except the last item.

As the waitress was about to leave, the customer said: "What about the kind word?" The waitress paused for a moment and replied: "Don't eat that egg."

A story is told of an old poacher in a hill village who was lying seriously ill and was called upon one day by his veteran enemy, the gamekeeper.

Almost at his last gasp, the poacher consented to be reconciled to the gamekeeper and a touching scene followed in which both men shook hands in mutual forgiveness.

The gamekeeper was greatly affected and had tears in his eyes as he left the old man's room. At the door he was called back, and the old poacher, raising himself in bed, gasped: "But thou mun remember, Fred, if Ah should 'appen to get better, all this is off."

The conversation in the inn at Howden turned to haircutting.

"Ah allus cuts me own," said one old character, to the amazement of the assembled company.

"How on earth do you reach?" came the incredulous question.

"Oh, Ah reaches all right," came the answer. "Ah stands on a chair."

Two old men were discussing the respective sizes of their large families. "Aye," said one. "I'd eleven, all lasses. I'd 'ave liked a cricket team but Ah got a sewing class."

Squire to old Dalesman who lived on his estate, in a two-roomed cottage, alone with a billy-goat:

"Isn't there rather a smell?"

Dalesman: "Bless you sir, billy's larnt to put up wi that."

The doctor had called to see a railway signalmen who had been off duty with rheumatism. After examining him the doctor remarked: "It would be a good thing if you took a bath before you retire."

"Nay," said the railwayman. "That's a long time to wait. Ah don't retire for another ten years."

Sheffield man to his pal in the Lake District: "There's nowt here but scenery."

An old man had joined in the dances at the village hall and Lizzie, equally elderly, had whizzed him round frantically. The old man stopped suddenly and said: "Lizzie, can't we reverse?"

"Why, is ta gettin' dizzy, Sam?"

"Nay," said Sam, "but tha's unscrewing me wooden leg."

In a Yorkshire town lived two brothers, in business as coal dealers, and their reputation for honest dealing was not of the highest. One of the brothers who started to attend church meetings, became 'converted' and then set about to reform his kith and kin. In the end it came to a showdown.

The other brother, quite exasperated, retorted thus: "Nah, look here owd chap. It's all vary well for thee to talk, but Ah'm baan to ask thi a straight question: If Ah get converted, who does ta think's baan to weight t' coil?"

"There's nowt 'ere but scenery."

An old fishing enthusiast from Bradford journeyed the banks of the Wharfe. He thought this was an ideal place to catch a mess of trout.

His reverie was suddenly disturbed by the crunch of footsteps. A stranger approached him. "Now, my man, do you know you are trespassing on private grounds and fishing in private waters?"

The old fisherman replied: "Noa, Ah didn't knaw I wor doing owt wreng."

Pulling out his fishing line and relighting his pipe, he added: "An' who's tha?"

As he walked slowly away the stranger replied: "I am the Duke of Devonshire. All the waters and land are my private property."

"Nay, Duke," said the angler, "tha's all wreng. Thy waters are through t'brig by nah. An' tha said all the lands wur thine. Ha did tha git 'em?"

"I received them from my ancestors."

"Ha did they git 'em?"

"They fought for them."

With a twinkle in his eye, the fisherman retorted: "Well, I'll feight thee for 'em."

Mrs Briggs looked across at Mrs Stoney.

"Go ahead, lass, an' hev another piece o' cake."

"No, thanks," was the reply. "I've had three already."

"Tha's hed four," said Mrs Briggs, "but you're welcome to another piece, lass."

Grandpa was dying, and his wife, having to leave him alone while she went to the shop, turned out the light.

"We mun save wer brass, lad," she told him.

"Tha'll leave me a candle?" he begged.

"Well – all reight – but if tha feels thissen goin', blow it aht."

A North Riding farmer decided to sell his mare and buy a motor. So he approached another farmer on market day.

"Would ter like to mak' me an offer for 'er, Tom?"

"Oh. Ah doan't knaw. Wo't she like?"

"Oh. She's all reight. She's a good worker: good on t' collar, an' quiet; only she doesn't look so well."

After a brief inspection Tom agreed to buy it, but a couple of days later he was back with the mare and in a state of high indigination.

"Wot's ter mean by palmin' off a 'oss like this 'ere on me?" he demanded. "T' mare's blind."

"Nay," was the reply, "Ah telled thi she didn't look so well."

A careless motorist had just crashed into a telephone pole in Wensleydale. Wires, pole, everything came down around his ears. As rescuers untangled him from the wreckage, he reached out feebly, fingered the wires and murmured: "Thank heaven I lived clean. They've given me a harp."

At the annual farmers' dinner an old Dalesman was offered Gorgonzola cheese, and took a piece. After a close inspection, he put it in his mouth, chewed it, and spat it out.

"Have you never tasted it before?" he was asked.

"No, nivver tasted such stuff afore," was the reply, "but I've trod in it."

A farmer from the Dales was admitted to hospital suffering from severe pains.

When asked where he had the pains his reply was: "I mostly gets 'em i t' pigsty."

Salesman selling suitcase to Yorkshireman: "Shall I wrap it up for you, sir?"

"Nay, lad, just put t' paper an' string inside."

A Leeds housewife had friends to tea. She went into the pantry but came out empty handed and said: "Nay, A've fergitten what a'went for. A'm as bad as our George. 'E once 'ad to do a fortnit i' Armley jail, an' when 'e cum out e'd to ask mi mother what we called t' cat."

Pat, the haytime man, went to a village to make inquiries about having his boots repaired.
Pat: "How much do you charge for front soling?"
Cobbler: "7s 9d."
Pat: "How much for heeling?"
Cobbler: "2s 9d."
Pat: "Ah, you can heel mine right up to the toe."

A boy got into a crowded train and placed a picnic basket on the luggage rack. From it drops began to fall on to the bald head of a posh man from the city. He, feeling somewhat embarrassed, ventured: "Do you mind removing that pork pie from the rack?"
"That's no pork pie, it's a pup."

A Dales household received a supply of electricity but used less than a unit during the quarter. "You're very economical," the meter inspector remarked after jotting down details of the quarter's usage.
"Nay, it's not that," the dear old lady of the house replied. "We nobbut put t' leets on so as to find our way to t' paraffin lamp."

During the bombardment of Whitby by units of the German Navy in December 1914, two women took refuge behind a boulder.
"Dizzn't tha think we'd better pray?" suggested one.
"Hod hard a bit," was the reply. "Let's see what happens first."

Two chaps were having a talk about old times. One of them said: "Does tha know when Ah wor young Ah wor reight ugly."

The other looked at him a minute and then said: "By gum, tha's kept thi youth weel."

A Dales farmer went into an ironmonger's shop to have a key cut from a pattern he brought with him. When the key was ready the shopkeeper handed it to him.

Farmer: "Will t' key be o'reight now?"

Shopkeeper: "Yes, it will."

Farmer: "Well, I hope it fits, because t' other 'un didn't."

At a South Yorkshire hospital clinic a young lady was among the blood donors.

The nurse asked her if she knew her type.

"Oh, yes," she said. "I'm the passionate type."

"This," said a salesman in a West Riding market, "is a universal solvent. It will dissolve anything."

"By gow, it sounds all reet," said a listener. "But I wonder what yon chap keeps it in."

The shopkeeper and an old Dales farmer were discussing the St Leger.

"So yer picked a slow un, eh?" the shopkeeper asked.

"Well, Ah wouldn't say he was slow," the farmer said, "but t' jockey took a packed lunch."

Many years ago, in a rural district, a farmer was helping at the delivery of his latest offspring by holding the oil lamp. When the doctor had produced not one but two fine babies, the farmer bolted out of the room. "Come back with that lamp," shouted the doctor.

"I will not," was his answer. "It's t' light that's attracting 'em."

Two Dalesmen on holiday hired a boat for lake fishing, and had no success for several hours. Then suddenly at one spot the water seemed alive with fish, and they dragged them out at great speed.

As they were rowing towards the landing, one of the anglers remarked: "Ah hope tha marked t' spot whear we got all o' them fish."

The other nodded. "Aye, Ah put a cross on t' bottom o' t' boat."

"Tha gurt fooil," shouted the first, "we might not get t' same boat tomorrow."

A comment on his wife's pastry: "Tha could shoe hosses wi' it."

The old dame was full of the local gossip, particularly of a set-to she'd just had with a 'Lady Jane type wi' edging on' who she 'couldn't abide', and who was 'jumped-up an' too nice to skin onions'. The old dame ended her description of this 'mimsy-finicky' creature with: "Ay, shoo's one o' that soort that gooas lookin' for lice i' bald heeads."

At the cosmetic counter in a large department store in Sheffield, an old lady asked the price of a well-known brand of perfumed soap.

On being told, she exclaimed: "Eh lass, I'd want a new face for that price, not just a clean one."

Ben was a minder in a Bradford mill and was well-known for his parsimonious habits, never having been known to have a day off work.

One afternoon his workmates noticed him looking frequently out of the window. When asked the reason Ben replied: "Nay, Ah war only watchin' fur t' funeral. They're buryin' t' wife today, tha knows."

A traveller found two Dales laddies sobbing bitterly by the side of a dead donkey in a frost-bitten field.

"Were you very fond of the animal?" he enquired.

"No," replied one of the lads. "But we've got to bury it."

It was the annual feast at a West Riding town, and before a crowded audience at the menagerie the lady lion tamer was allowing the lion to take pieces of sugar from her lips.

The audience was spellbound, but one man, differently constituted from the rest, suddenly broke the silence with the contemptous: "That's easy."

"Oh," challenged another, "and could you do it?"

"Aye, of course," was the reply. "Just as easy as t' lion."

At Hull they tell this story of a night of very dense fog when the junior officer on the ship's bridge was becoming more and more rattled.

As he stared ahead trying to pierce the gloom, he saw a dim figure leaning over a rail some yards from the ship's prow.

"What do you think you're doing with your ship?" he roared. "Don't you know the elementary rules of seamanship?"

"This ship isn't a ship," came the reply. "This is a lighthouse."

Years ago pigeon fanciers were numerous, and many races were organised. One character was taking some birds to the station (his entries for a race) when he met an acquaintance.

"Hello, Bill, sendin' thi pidgins off?" he queried.

"Aye."

"Ar monny is tu sendin'?"

"If tha guesses reight tha can hev 'em both."

"Tha's two," said the friend immediately.

"That isn't fair," said Bill. "Sum'dy's telled tha."

A visitor to a West Riding village was curious as to the meaning of a broad black mark high up the wall of the village pub.

"What does that mark stand for?" he asked.

"Oh, that was the height of the water in the big flood of 1893," he was told.

"Never. Why, the whole village and the whole county must have been yards under water."

"Well, no. You see the mark used to be about two feet off the ground, but as the boys kept rubbing it out, we had to put it higher."

A Dalesman summing up his sad situation: "Ay, that's life that is. God takes away yer teeth an' then he gives yer nuts."

A Craven farmer was asked what the weather would be. "Nay," he said. "Wi this Government in, owt could 'appen."

A West Riding farmer was regarding the ravages of a flood.

"Kit," called a neighbour. "Ah've just seen all your pigs washed down t' river."

"What about Robinson's pigs?" asked the farmer.

"Oh, they're gone too."

"And Calvert's?"

"Oh, aye, they've gone."

"Ah, well," said the farmer, cheering up. "Maybe it isn't as bad as Ah thowt."

Through a Dales doorway a woman was heard rebuking a careless daughter: "Broke yer father's saucer, 'ave yer? Well, Ah don't know what 'e'll say when 'e has to drink out of 'is cup."

A young girl asked an old lady in the village how she was managing the new decimal money. Her reply was: "Ee, I'm noan botherin' lass; it'll not catch on in aar village."

Two mates who had joined at a football pool coupon were lucky one week and bought a couple of horses. " 'Ow are we bahn to know which owns which?" queried one. The other replied: "We'll cut my horse's tail short." Some lads got into the stable and cut the other horse's tail short, too.

When they saw the animals next night one said: "Well, we're flummaxed agean." So they decided to cut one horse's mane short. Again the boys cut the other horse's mane short, too. They were baffled, until one hit on a solution. "Ah'll tell thi what," he explained. "Tha mun tak white 'un, and Ah'll tak black 'un."

He was stopped in the street one day by a man who inquired: "Is it true that thou art mayor of this 'ere town?"

The alderman acknowledged that he was.

"Eh, well," replied the inquirer with true Yorkshire bluntness, "we get all sooarts, don't we?"

It was market day in a Yorkshire town. Two farmers having carried out a business deal went into the village inn to seal the transaction with a drink. Suddenly two men burst in and announced:

"This is a hold-up."

Quick as lightning, one of the farmers stuck something into his friend's pocket, saying: "Here Fred, take this."

"What is it?" whispered Fred.

"The £10 I owe you," he replied.

Norman was a member of an originally large family. His pal said to him: "I was sorry to hear you lost your brother, Len, last week."

He replied: "Ah well, it comes to all on us. I said to mi sister after t' funeral, 'Well, Betsy lass, ther's only me and thee left nah, and thar's not lookin' too well.' "

The new inmate in Armley Jail was surprised to see he would be sharing a cell with a vicar, who explained: "I fought the temptations of the flesh my whole life through."

"So what are you doing in jail then, Reverend?"

"I said I fought them...I didn't say I won."

Two old chaps were talking together after a funeral, and one said: "By gow, thee an' me have been attending funerals for well over fifty years. We started way back with t' old black coach, and now we're up in t' Rolls Royce next to t' hearse."

"We hev an' all," said his pal. "But Ah doan't want onny further promotion."

The midwife warned the expectant father: "Always remember that the first three minutes of life are most dangerous."

He replied: "The last three are a bit dodgy as well."

The funeral procession was passing through the village, and the old gardener, who was a pal of the deceased, felt somewhat neglected.

"Sham' on yer," he called, shaking his fist. "Sham' on yer. If 'e'd a' bin alive, Ah'd 'a' bin t' very fust 'e'd 'ave asked."

Sam, who kept the local sausage shop, was taken ill and died. His friend Tommy was invited to the funeral, and afterwards he and the other mourners went back to Sam's widow's house for something to eat.

As sausage was the easiest to cook, she asked the mourners if they would like some. Tommy didn't seem satisfied, and so Sam's widow asked him: "Mebbe sausage don't agree with you, Tommy – is there owt else you'd like?"

"Well," replied Tommy. "Ah've nowt ageean sausage, but Ah think 'at black puddin' would be more appropriate for a funeral."

"Well, according to t' Bible, Malta's left at t' whale spout."

A farmer up the dale was also the gravedigger at Chapel-le-Dale Church.

One day, when he had just completed the difficult task of digging a grave in the rocky ground, a sightseer approached him from a motor car.

"I say, my man," said the tourist, "that's not a very deep grave you've dug."

This irritated the weary farmer a little.

"No," said he, "but there's noan on 'em gitten out yet."

He was complaining how besotted his friend was with his new wife: "If she asked him to bring her Semerwater in a saucepan, he'd do it."

Old man, to his cronies in the pub:

"I 'eard owd Tom's deed sudden."

"Oh. 'Ow owd were he?"

"Near on eighty-two."

"That's noan so sudden."

A North Country skipper had to deliver an Admiralty vessel from Hull to Malta just after the First World War.

He arrrived in good order, but several weeks late. The naval officer who had issued the instructions had worked out the probable time of the passage and could not understand the delay. So he asked a Fleet Navigating Officer to investigate.

The officer asked to see the log.

"Bless you, sir, I don't keep a log," said the skipper.

"Then can I see your charts?" asked the officer.

But there were no charts, either.

"But how did you find your way to Malta at all?" queried the puzzled officer.

"Ah," said the skipper. "You see I've got a Bible wi' maps at t' back of it."

Some years ago, in the cinema of a mining village in South Yorkshire, a veiled figure in deep black came in, followed by what appeared to be an entire funeral party.

She handed the usherette the sheaf of tickets and, noting her look of surprise, said solemnly: "Ee lass, my Jack never did care for 'am teas but he reight enjoyed a cowboy picture."

The conversation in a Wensleydale inn centred upon whose funeral was taking place in the churchyard opposite.

"Ah'll tell tha who it is, it's yon chap from next village who allus sat in't same corner when 'ee come in't bar."

"Dost tha mean chap who allus had plenty to say about women?"

"Aye, that's reet."

"Well I'm blowed, is he dead?"

"Why, Ah don't know about that, but they're burying 'im."

An East Riding farmer had attended the funeral of a farmer in the next Wolds village. He returned home, eased himself into a chair by the kitchen fire, and announced with a smile of satisfaction: "Well, we've got him sided."

Old Sam was sadly out of sorts, so his family sent for the doctor.

"My good man," the doctor said. "Unless you give up drinking at once, you will be blind."

Old Sam pondered a while and then replied: "Ah'm gettin old. Ah've been to St Leger at Doncaster, Ah've seen York Minster, and Ah've visited Bridlington. There's nowt much left to see. Ah'll risk it."

An old lady made a habit of going into the churchyard each day. A friend could not understand why she did this. She was told: "Ah lass, you can't believe what a grand feeling it is to be able to walk out again at eighty."

It was a bitterly cold winter's night. The barber had closed his shop and, with an elderly lady, battled his way through the snow to a remote cottage 'to shave Joe'. As they reached the cottage door, she asked: "So 'ow much do yer charge for shavin', like?"

"Oh, a tanner for an old customer like Joe," replied the barber. "We've missed him, yer know. 'As he not been so well?"

"No, 'E 'asn't – he died this morning," said the elderly lady.

"Oh well, that's different. It's allus awf-a-crahn for shavin' a stiff-un."

"Awf-a-crahn," cried the lady, aghast. "Well, Ah doan't think Ah'll bother – it's not as if he's goin' anywheer particular."

Old George is a retired Dales farmer. Recently the conversation turned to the death of one of his cronies, who had had the reputation of being somewhat stingy.

"I'm told that old Harry left £5,000," his visitor remarked admiringly.

"That he didn't," George said.

His visitor expressed surprise.

"Harry left no money," he went on. "He was taken from it."

John and Mary were an old couple who lived in a cottage outside Leeds. John was bedridden for many years and was slowly sinking.

Near the end the doctor came and with Mary stood by the bed looking at the old man. There was little movement, and the doctor turned to the old lady and remarked: "Well, Mary dear, I think John has almost gone."

John, however, opened one eye and said: "Nay, doctor, not joost yet."

To which Mary replied: "Thoo be quiet, John. T' doctor knaws better than thee."

Sam, a Yorkshire sexton, was digging a grave. It was well away from all others in the churchyard. He was deeply engrossed in the work when a man approached and stood by the mound of earth which Sam had thrown out. He coughed. Sam looked up. "Wot dosta want, lad?" he queried.

"Ah were nobbut wonderin'," replied the visitor, "why tha's diggin' this 'ere grave so far from t' others."

"Well," said Sam, "it's like this 'ere. This chap 'as nobut lived 'ere a twelve munth, an' this is wheer Ah puts t' oddments."

Heard in a Halifax greengrocer's shop:

"I want some grapes for a sick friend. What are those?"

"They're £2 a bunch."

"Oh, he's not as sick as all that."

Harry was busy with the spring redecoration of one of the rooms in his house, and recalling something he had done a few months earlier, put his hat on and went to the home of one of his friends a few streets away and tapped on the door. Asking the lady who answered his knock: "Is Bill in?" he was somewhat taken aback when the woman said: "'Aven't you 'eard – Bill died – it were his funeral last week." Nonplussed by the news Harry paused for a few moments before saying "Ee, Ah'm iver so sorry." Then after a slight pause continued: "Did 'e say owt about a pot of white paint?"

Jack had been ill for some time but he was making a good recovery and was sent to Scarborough by his doctor for a week's convalescence. Unfortunately towards the end of the week he suffered a relapse and suddenly died. His body was taken home and, as the relatives stood round the coffin paying their last respects and consoling his widow, his sister turned to her and said: "Ee lass, but he's a lovely colour – that week in Scarborough did him a world of good."

" 'As tha got any special offers on grapes –
Ah'm 'ospital visitin' and me pal's only a little bit sick."

Maggie's husband Roland had died suddenly, and a small group of neighbours called round to offer condolences to the bereaved lady.

"Whatever happened, Maggie?" said one. "He allus seemed such a big strong 'ealthy chap."

The widow replied:

"Well, I were gettin' t' Sunday dinner on and told 'im to go and cut a cabbage out o't gardin. 'E were gone ever so long, so I went down to see what 'e were doin' and found 'im laid among the cabbages – stone deead."

"Eee, what a terrible shock it must 'ave bin," exclaimed another lady. "Whatever did you do?"

"Well," said the widow, wiping away a tear. "I 'ad to open a tin of peas."

An old roadsman was leaning against the churchyard wall coughing violently as a friend passed. He paused a moment and said how sorry he was to hear him.

"Aye," he said, when he got his breath back. "Ah'm in a bad way, but ther's plenty o' folk over this 'ere wall as 'ud be glad o' this cough."

The undertaker, having been upstairs to take the measurements, joined the silent group sitting round the fire in a Wensleydale farmhouse. He was passed the whisky and, having had a nip, waited a few minutes before asking: "When sall we bury 'm?"

A long pause, then the widow said:

"Hoo aboot next Frida?"

"Aye. That'll be all reet."

Another long silence, then the eldest son, said:

"No that weean't do."

"Why?"

"T' bull sale at 'Awes."

An old Dalesman took a morbid delight in looking in the 'deaths' column of the local newspaper every week, and noting the passing away of members of his former wide acquaintance. "There's a lot on 'em goin' this winter," he told the crony. "There wor owd Silas Butterfield t' week afoor last, an' there's Benny Ackroyd this week. It gi's me a funny feelin' ter look i' t' paper an' see who's died."

"Ay," said his crony. "An' it'll not allus be sumbody else."

Two elderly Dalesmen in Leyburn marketplace were discussing the serious ailment of a third.

"Aye," said one, "Ah reckon only a post-mortem will show what it is."

"Maybe," replied the other, "but he's so weak he'd never stand that."

An infants teacher was showing her class round the church, and they arrived at the font which had a movable cover tapering to a point.

Before describing it she asked whether any child knew what it was.

One boy quickly spoke up and said: "A rocket, miss."

Sitting round the fireside one evening, Jim questioned his two young granddaughters about their school. They were delighted to tell him of their activities – of reading, writing, singing and 'nature'.

When questioned about arithmetic they asked if that was 'sums'. Having been assured that this was indeed the case, Alison, the younger, informed him that she didn't like 'takeways' because, she added, "sometimes you can't and then I forget to add one."

"Oh," said Susan, "takeaways are easy up to 'gozintas' because sometimes they won't go."

At a rugby league match, two veteran supporters had their own views on a decision of the referee.

"Of course he wor offside!" yelled one.

"How could he be?" retorted the other.

All their knowledge of the rules of the game was brought to bear in the ensuing argument. Finally, having had enough, the second came in with:

"Alreet, then, thou sez he wor offside and Ah doan't reckon he wor, so us'll agree to differ, that's all."

"Oh no we woan't," came the emphatic rejoinder. "Ah'm not differing wi ye, cos Ah knoa Ah'm reet."

North Country old timer's reply to inquiry about his health: "Still kicking but nut raising much dust."

A note found in a library book: "Joe, when you've read up to here, please take the pie out of the oven."